KU-850-273

Contents

Using e-books and e-readers for adult learning

With a focus on adult literacy

Sandie Gay • Tina Richardson

niace

promoting adult learning

49926

Published by the National Institute of Adult Continuing Education
NIACE (England and Wales)
21 De Montfort Street
Leicester LE1 7GE

Company registration no. 2603322
Charity registration no. 1002775

The National Institute of Adult Continuing Education (NIACE) is an independent charity
which promotes adult learning across England and Wales. Through its research,
development, publications, events, outreach and advocacy activity, NIACE works to
improve the quality and breadth of opportunities available for all adults so they can
benefit from learning throughout their lives.

www.niace.org.uk

For details of all our publications, visit http://shop.niace.org.uk

Follow NIACE on Twitter: @NIACEhq
@NIACEDC (Wales)
@NIACEbooks (Publications)

Cataloguing in Publications Data
A CIP record for this title is available from the British Library

978-1-86201-609-5 (Print)
978-1-86201-610-1 (PDF)
978-1-86201-611-8 (ePub)
978-1-86201-612-5 (Kindle)
978-1-86201-613-2 (Online)

All websites referenced in this book were correct and accessible at the time of going to
press.

Printed in the UK by Latimer Trend & Company Ltd
Designed and typeset by Book Production Services, London

Introduction

> "If creating lifelong readers is the goal, then every tool is needed."
> *Kylene Beers[1]*

This book focuses on using e-book and e-reader technology in the adult classroom. It will serve as a guide for the teacher or curriculum leader who is familiar with and may own their own e-reading device. They may have even used e-readers in the classroom already, but perhaps need more suggestions on their use. Similarly, it can be used as a guide for a teacher or curriculum leader who has never owned or used an e-reader, but is interested in their application in the adult education classroom. The overall intention of this book is to provide a guide on what different e-reading devices and e-books can offer the learner for the advancement of their learning, and to outline some of the issues and challenges that come with using them in the adult classroom.

An obvious use for e-readers and e-books is to encourage emergent readers to gain a pleasure in reading and using the technologies to advantage for facilitating the development of their literacy skills. Therefore, at various points in the book, we have highlighted how specific functions of e-readers and other multi-function devices that can be used to read digital books lend themselves to these purposes. We provide a whole chapter on practical, easy to implement, suggested uses in the literacy classroom (see *Chapter 7*). We also list some free software that you and your learners can use to create your own e-books and suggest how you can get them published (see *Chapter 6*). You can even publish them to sell! We

---

1. See http://interactivereadalouds.pbworks.com/f/Listen+While+You+Read.pdf for source.

hope these ideas work for you and we would love to hear from you about further uses of e-readers and e-books that we can share with others (contact us at: sandie.gay@gmail.com and t.a.richardson@staffs.ac.uk).

There is a chapter on access and accessibility (see *Chapter 3*) which looks at the functions and features that can help bring the pleasure of reading to learners who experience difficulties reading print, but we also consider some of the limitations of these technologies here.

Finally, there's a call to action! You can get involved in helping inform future developments in e-books and e-readers for adult learning (see *Conclusion*).

One note of caution: e-readers and the various devices that support e-books are developing at an incredibly rapid rate. Please refer to the manufacturers' websites for up-to-date information about the cost and technical specifications of particular ones, as well as new devices that may be coming on the market in the near future.

CHAPTER 1
What are e-books?

An electronic book (e-book) is just another way of accessing a book; it is a digital way of reading that means that some e-books can be quite interactive – in a way that a paper version cannot be. However, not all e-books are interactive. Even an interactive e-book, depending on the e-reader on which you are reading it, may or may not be able to use all of that interactivity. Understanding something about the different kinds of e-books available can help you choose what kind of e-reader you want to use in the classroom.

The Oxford Dictionary of English defines an e-book as a 'digital version of a printed book', so an e-book can be seen as just another version of a book. However, this definition, while helpful, is a little old fashioned, as some e-books may never have been available as a printed book – they may only exist as digital versions.

To be able to read an e-book written in an e-book format requires software installed on a device to show the contents of the e-book. The software can run on three types of platform:

‣ e-book readers (dedicated and hybrid);

‣ standard computer or laptop; and

‣ mobile devices – such as smartphones and tablets (multifunctional devices).

An e-book is made up of words (and pictures) that must be read with a computer or some kind of e-reader or software application on a multifunctional device. At a basic level, an e-book could just be a PDF (portable document format) of a published book. This is often true of free books that are out of copyright; basically the pages of the physical book have been reproduced in electronic form. The interactivity will then only come from the e-reader – for example, search options and text to speech. Some e-books have been created specifically to be read in a digital format and have extra interactive features, such as moving pictures, sounds to coincide with the action in the text, and hyperlinks to allow you to find out more information about a highlighted topic. However, it is important to remember that, although an e-book may have many levels of interactivity, if your e-reader does not have those features, then you will not be able to use them. The easiest way of getting an e-book is by downloading it to your e-reader. For multifunctional devices, you will need to download an appropriate application (or 'app') which will then let you read e-books on your device (see *Chapter 3* for more information).

Often the format in which an e-book has been created will limit you to the device on which you can then read that e-book. A good example of this is the Kindle. This e-reader has been produced so that you can only download e-books from the Amazon website (widening out to Waterstones). All good websites that you can download e-books from will explain what format they are in and the device you can read the e-book on. There are pieces of software, such as Calibre, that you can download and which can convert text into whatever format you need for your e-reader, but having to convert a document can be time consuming. The most widely supported format is .EPUB, which most devices can read, except, notably, the Kindle.

There is another way of looking at e-books – that of creating books, short stories, instructions and so on – and downloading them to an e-reader (please refer to the GABES case study in *Chapter 4*). Again, pieces of software can be used, such as Mobipocket eBook Creator, which will convert your documents into a format suitable for download to an e-reader. You can even sell them (please refer to *Chapter 7* for more information).

E-books in different languages

As a way of encouraging learners who do not have English as a first language, it may be appropriate for them to use an e-book device to read books in their own language until they feel more comfortable using the technology. This will allow the student to use strategies that they have for reading in their own language and, hopefully, when they attempt to read something in English on an e-reader they will carry those same strategies over to help them decode the language.

Some of the websites that offer free e-books in the English language also offer them in other languages. For example, Project Gutenberg[2] offers books in over 50 languages. However, only the first ten languages provide any significant choice of over 100 books; the rest have an average of about ten books in each language.

TIP!

The best way to find books in different languages is to look on the Internet for websites from the appropriate countries that sell or offer free e-books. Alternatively, you could get a student who is fluent in that language to search for them. A quick look on the German version of Amazon[3] will reveal 'gratis Kindle e-books' for you to click on and search in the Kindle section.

2. See www.gutenberg.org for more information.
3. www.amazon.de

There is another aspect to digital reading that we have not looked at: e-journals, e-magazines and e-newspapers. Most of these are paid-for subscriptions that can be delivered to an e-reader on a daily, weekly or monthly basis, depending on the subscription.

Many major publications offer a digital version that can be read on a laptop or PC, or sent to your e-reader. You can also take out a subscription through an aggregator such as Amazon. In Britain, Amazon offers the largest number of e-journals, e-magazines and e-newspapers on one site from Britain and beyond.

There are free e-journals, e-magazines and e-newspapers from around the world, but most of it is paid-for content. One thing you need to consider is how your e-magazine or e-newspaper is going to display on an e-reader. If the e-magazine you want to read is in full colour then it may not display well on a greyscale e-reader. From an interactive colour point of view, an e-reader may not always be the best device to read an e-newspaper or e-magazine on. However, if that is the only device you have, it is perfectly fine; perhaps you just need to think about how learners will read a digital e-newspaper compared to a paper version. The skimming and scanning techniques that you would normally use with learners to choose a story to read are not really possible with an e-newspaper or e-magazine on a dedicated e-reader.

If you want your learners to read mainly e-newspapers and e-magazines, then perhaps a dedicated e-reader is not the best option – you may need to consider a tablet or a multifunctional device. Many publications offer a free app so that you can read an e-newspaper or e-magazine on a tablet or multifunctional device, but you may need to subscribe to be able to read the publication.

For some ideas about using e-journals, e-magazines and e-newspapers in the classroom, please refer to *Chapter 7* on suggested uses.

TIP!

To get an idea of the viability of reading a magazine or e-newspaper on a dedicated e-reader, many sites offer 14-day free trials of the e-journals, e-magazines and e-newspapers. All you need to do is cancel the subscription before the trial is over and you will not need to pay.

CHAPTER 2
What are e-readers and e-book apps?

This chapter reviews some basic features of e-readers and multifunctional devices that can be used to read e-books, and highlights considerations for learning providers thinking about investing in this technology. Additionally, we provide suggestions, where appropriate, on how specific features may be useful in developing learners' literacy skills.

Dedicated e-readers

At a basic level, a dedicated e-reader is a portable, pocket-sized device specifically designed for reading e-books, e-newspapers, documents and e-magazines (please see *Chapter 1* for an overview of e-books). Generally, the size of an e-reader equates to the size of a normal paperback book, only much thinner. The e-reading screen displays a page or two of a book at a time and you can turn to the next page by pressing a button or swiping the screen.

Multifunctional devices

You can buy dedicated e-readers, where the main function is to be able to read books, or multifunctional devices – like smartphones and tablets – where being able to read e-books is just one of the many things that the device can do.

Using the Kindle app on an iPad

Hybrid devices

There are also hybrid devices such as the Kindle Fire and the Kobo Vox, which are dedicated e-readers that are also capable of displaying colour and playing videos. They can support apps that allow you to email or play games.

Note: Unless referring specifically to dedicated e-readers or multifunctional devices, the generic term 'e-readers' will be used to refer to the hardware on which the e-book can be read. Other technical words can be found in the Glossary later in the book.

Example of a hybrid device: the Kindle Fire

E-reader features

The table that follows considers different e-reader features and how they can be used to advantage by learners. A cross-referenced table to show which e-readers from the top three brands available in the UK (Amazon, Sony and Kobo) include the features discussed is available as an Appendix at the back of the book. This table also looks at the popular Apple iPad as an example of a tablet, and iPod and smartphones as examples of the smaller multifunctional devices that can all be used as alternative e-book reading devices (please refer to the GABES case study in *Chapter 4*). In the next section of this chapter, we also consider e-book reading apps used for accessing e-books on multifunctional devices and provide a review of some of the popular ones.

There are many e-readers and multifunctional devices on the market of varying sizes, capabilities and costs, so it's not possible to review them all. Searching on the Internet will uncover just as many comparisons, reviews and opinions about the best devices as there are devices. As with all technology, you will probably not find one device that does all you want, and you will need to compromise, but we hope the information here will help inform your decision-making process.

Feature	Detail	Considerations and tips for use in the classroom or learning activities
Physical		
1 **Screen size**	Dedicated e-readers usually have a screen size between five and seven inches. Multifunctional, portable e-book reading devices, like Apple's iPad, have screen sizes of up to ten inches. A laptop usually has a screen size of up to 17 inches.	It is difficult to say which screen size is optimal for comfortable reading. The bigger ones are obviously easier to read on, but if portability is high on your list of priorities, then the smaller devices will suit you better due to their size, and as they tend to be lighter too.

If your device is mostly to be stored and used in your classroom, then portability may be less of an issue, and going for the larger screen size is preferable.

The bigger screen sizes are available on multifunctional devices (often referred to as tablets), so have other functions worth considering, with the most significant of these being web browsing and access to other apps.

If you need to compromise on screen size against portability (for example, if you are working in a community venue), then remember that e-readers offer several font sizes to make reading text easier on a small screen. |

Feature	Detail	Considerations and tips for use in the classroom or learning activities
Physical		
2 **Screen type** Refer to the Newcastle City Learning case study and analysis in Chapter 4	There are two types to consider – the e-ink screens such as those on the dedicated e-readers like the Kindle or Sony Reader, or the LCD/LED ones such as on the Kobo Vox, iPad or smartphones. The e-ink screens, especially designed to make text look like print, are glare-free, allowing the text to be visible and sharply in focus even in bright, reflective light (for example, in sunlight), and readable even when held at a slight angle (not face-on). The LCD/LED screens do reflect, and in bright sunshine the glare often means that you cannot see the text.	The e-ink screens of the dedicated e-readers are very pleasant and easy to read from, simulating the experience of reading a physical book or document. The Kobo Vox e-reader supports colour too, so it's great for photos and images in books such as cookbooks, travel guides, comics and magazines, and e-newspapers – all excellent resources to support literacy development. The glare of the multifunctional devices can make reading for any length of time hard on the eyes, causing fatigue. However, use for learning development activities is likely to be intermittent rather than for prolonged reading, and if your intended use is mainly in the classroom, then glare is less of an issue anyway. Also, the back-lighting feature of the LCD screens can be useful indoors if light is low; for example, at some community venues. The setting for the brightness can be adjusted to suit and help reduce the tiring effect on the eyes.

Feature	Detail	Considerations and tips for use in the classroom or learning activities
Physical		
3 **Screen orientation**	Most e-readers allow you to view text in portrait or landscape view – this alters how much text you can see on the screen and on one line.	To be able to view the page text in vertical (portrait) or horizontal (landscape) view can be helpful in supporting literacy exercises for learners – for example, if you are working at sentence level and you can see the whole sentence in one line by simply changing the orientation (without necessitating a change in the font size). This can help the learner to focus on understanding the structure of the sentence.
4 **Single-page or double-page screen view**	You normally have an option to see a single page or two pages on screen. The e-book reading apps, available for use on e-book reading devices such as the iPad or computer, allow two pages to be viewed at once. Of the e-readers reviewed, the Kobo Vox also offers this feature.	This is a nice feature that allows a more authentic experience of reading a book. Simulating the experience of reading a book can develop transferable concepts of reading from devices to physical books for learners who are yet to develop a reading habit.
5 **Page turning** Refer to the GABES case study and analysis in Chapter 4	Generally, there are two ways in which pages are turned, depending on the type of e-reader – those with touch screens are swiped or tapped; those without have forward and back buttons to click.	Consider the needs of your learners, as the tactile click bars can be helpful for some with visual difficulties, but perhaps not for learners with motor disabilities, and vice versa for touch-screen turning.

Feature	Detail	Considerations and tips for use in the classroom or learning activities
Physical		
6 **Text input**	Most e-readers have a virtual keyboard which is used either by touch (such as Kindle Touch, Kobo Touch, iPad or smartphones) or using button pads/joysticks built into the frame (such as Kobo WiFi). The Sony Reader has a touchscreen input and includes a stylus to help with accurate tapping. The Kindle Keyboard has a physical keyboard plus buttons for moving the cursor on the screen.	Multifunction devices with touch-screen turning can have authentic experience features designed in, such as simulation of an actual page being turned – a nice feature for transferring the learned concepts of reading a book. Using an onscreen keyboard requires a degree of accuracy, which should be a consideration if working with learners with visual impairments. Therefore a tactile keyboard, such as that on the Kindle Keyboard, may be more suitable. However, this same keyboard may be tricky for someone with arthritic fingers or other motor difficulties in the hands.
7 **Weight**	The dedicated e-book readers tend to be thinner and lighter in weight than the multifunctional devices.	A significant advantage if portability is high on your list of priorities; for example, many adult learning sessions are held in outreach environments and you are required to take kit with you. It is much easier to carry half a dozen e-readers than half a dozen laptops, or even half a dozen iPads. Weight may also be a consideration for some learners with specific conditions or physical disabilities (see Chapter 3 for more information).

	Feature	Detail	Considerations and tips for use in the classroom or learning activities
	Physical		
8	**Batteries and battery life**	E-readers and multifunctional devices contain rechargeable batteries and require mains power or USB chargers. In general, e-readers have a much longer battery life compared to multifunctional devices. In e-readers, the functions that use up battery power are changes of display, such as page turns (note, larger font sizes can mean more page turns), use of WiFi for downloading books or web browsing, and colour displays. In multifunctional devices, in normal use, the battery life is much shorter due to the processes that run in the background; for example, the back lighting for the screens uses up a lot of power.	For use in the classroom, you need a device that will be usable for the whole day at least, so charging up only needs to be done at the end of the day. Battery power is preserved in most devices by the power-down screen-saver option and can be further preserved in e-readers by switching on the WiFi only when needed. A secure place for leaving the device/s to be charged up is essential. If you are considering investing in several e-readers or other devices, a charging cabinet where they can all be plugged in and charged up overnight may be needed, adding to the cost. Batteries are usually good for many years but may need replacing eventually. However, costs need to be reviewed at this stage as it may be more cost-effective to renew the device itself.
9	**Charge-up time**	Different devices require different amounts of time to fully charge up.	Along with the power duration, the time taken to fully charge up devices is an important consideration in order to manage scheduling the use of the devices in classroom learning activities.

Feature	Detail	Considerations and tips for use in the classroom or learning activities
Built-in software functions		
10 **Web browsing (connection type)** Refer to the GABES case study and analysis in Chapter 4	Most e-readers include WiFi to enable you to download e-books via the device, and weren't designed for normal web browsing, which can be very slow and therefore impair the user experience. With boundaries blurring between e-readers and multifunctional devices, manufacturers are improving this function in an attempt to meet user demand; for example, Kobo Vox is designed for emails, running apps and social networking, and the Kindle Touch is trialling a new type of browser based on WebKit for a better browsing experience.	Ensuring portable digital devices are charged up for use can be the bane of learning providers' lives, and often a barrier to use of mobile technology in the classroom. When not being used for downloading books, WiFi should be switched off to preserve battery power. The advantages of multifunctional devices, web-browsing, emails, apps and games mean that you have a flexible device for many uses and access to web resources too, but the downside is that these functions can lead to distractions for learners. Web browsing, playing games and running apps means that power is much more quickly used up, so the devices need to be charged up more often.
11 **E-book format supported**	E-books are published in a variety of formats and not all formats are supported by all e-readers. The main categories are: Open standards format – .EPUB and .PDF – most e-readers support this.	A significant consideration when investing in e-readers is the availability of e-books in the appropriate format and cross-platform operability. Most e-readers (and their associated e-book reading apps) have opted to support the open standards .EPUB

Feature	Detail	Considerations and tips for use in the classroom or learning activities
Built-in software functions		
11 **E-book format supported (cont.)**	Proprietary format, restricted to specific brands of e-readers – for example, Amazon .AZW for the Kindle. Web formats – for example, .HTML, which requires a web browser.	format and so e-books in this format (unless DRM restricted*) can be read on any of these devices. Some e-readers have opted to read only a proprietary format, so can only be read on those specific devices. Kindles, for example, will read only the Kindle formats, .AZW or .MOBI. Generally, e-books in the unrestricted .EPUB format can be downloaded from any e-book store, transferred and read on any supporting device. The exception to this is the Apple iPad, which supports the .EPUB format, but e-books must be downloaded from its own e-book store in iTunes, and can only be read in its e-book app, iBooks. Native PDF e-books are supported by most e-readers, including the Kindle. DRM-restricted PDFs may need specific e-readers or e-book reading apps. *Digital Rights Management systems are used to restrict copying and distribution of an e-book among many other*

	Feature	Detail	Considerations and tips for use in the classroom or learning activities
	Built-in software functions		
	E-book format supported (cont.)		*restrictions, in order to protect the rights of authors, publishers and sellers, and this can have a big impact on the devices you choose to invest in (please refer to Chapter 3 for further information on DRM).*
12	**Supports multimedia files**	E-readers or other devices with speakers, e.g. the Kindle, Sony Reader, Kobo Vox or iPad can also be used with audio files; for example, MP3 or audiobook files such as Amazon's proprietary Audible format or the open .AAC format. Audio books can be downloaded and added to the e-reader in the same way as other document files. This is not strictly an e-reader function but provides the flexibility. Multifunctional devices, e.g. tablets and smartphones, will play and display most multimedia files and some hybrid e-readers, e.g. Kobo Vox, will play audio and video.	This will allow you to create and add voice files to the e-reader that learners can listen to as they read texts or carry out activities that you have loaded onto the e-reader. As multifunctional devices can play and display multimedia files, the e-books supported can be more interactive with embedded video and sound clips, and even games. All of these functions can enhance the reading experience, deepen understanding of topics and subjects, help engage and motivate struggling learners. Audio-books are read by real people (famously Stephen Fry in the Harry Potter books) giving the learner correct pronunciation of words, emphasis, tone, etc.

Feature	Detail	Considerations and tips for use in the classroom or learning activities
Built-in software functions		
13 **Ease of downloading books** Refer to the Stanmore College case study and analysis in Chapter 5	E-readers and e-book reading apps used on a tablet, smartphone or computer need to be registered with the associated e-book store; for example, Kindle e-readers and apps with Amazon, and Kobo e-readers and apps with the Kobo e-book store. 1)Most e-readers are WiFi enabled and support direct download from the associated e-book store to its library when in range of a WiFi network. Amazon offers 3G versions of the Kindle Keyboard and Kindle Touch, which uses a mobile network that allows download even when not in range of a WiFi network (but must be in range of the 3G network). 2)Direct download is possible from the associated e-book store to an e-book reading app on a connected computer, tablet or smartphone. Subsequently, these can be synchronised with other devices, including the e-reader itself, registered to the same account. 3)For all e-readers and e-book	E-readers need to be registered with the e-store from which you wish to buy your e-books, along with payment card details. Obviously, e-readers given to learners must be de-registered beforehand so learners are not able to buy books themselves on your account. E-book apps also need to be registered if you wish to use them for purchasing books through the link to the e-book store. It can be the same registration for both.

Feature	Detail	Considerations and tips for use in the classroom or learning activities
Built-in software functions		
13 **Ease of downloading books (cont.)**	reading apps, other than Amazon's Kindle and Kindle app, e-books in the .EPUB and .PDF format can also be downloaded from other e-book stores and libraries, and added by file transfer to the e-reader (by connecting it to the computer) and to the e-book reading app. E-books for the Kindle are available from Amazon's online store only (although, at the time of writing, talks were being held between Amazon and Waterstones to make Kindle e-books available from the Waterstones e-book store too).	
14 **Adding own documents** Refer to the Dudley College case study and analysis in Chapter 4 Refer to the GABES case study and analysis in Chapter 4	Most e-readers will allow you to add your own documents in PDF format by connecting the device to the computer and transferring a copy into the content folder. Amazon has a service that allows you to email the most popular document types (such as .DOC/.DOCX; .TXT; .RTF; .PDF, plus image files: .JPEG; .GIF; .PNG; .BMP) that you want your readers to be able to view on a Kindle. The	This feature has obvious benefits for use in the classroom because you can add your own exercise handouts and worksheets to the e-reader for your learners. Together with the highlighting/annotation facility, learners can carry out their learning activities and use the various accessibility features to suit their needs too.

Feature	Detail	Considerations and tips for use in the classroom or learning activities
Built-in software functions		
14 **Adding own documents (cont.)**	service converts the document to the Kindle e-book or .PDF format, and this appears in the book list. Additionally, you can download a 'Send to Kindle' add-on from Amazon (go to: www.amazon.com/gp/ feature.html/?docId= 1000719931) that lets you use this service easily by adding the option, 'Send to Kindle', to the right-click shortcut menu. When you want to send a document to the registered Kindle, right-click and select this option (available for a PC or Mac).	
15 **Text to speech**	Of the dedicated e-readers reviewed for this book, only the Kindle Touch and Keyboard for their books, e-newspapers, magazines and personal documents sent to the Kindle and Kobo Vox offer this feature. It must be noted that text to speech only works on e-books where this feature has been enabled in the DRM coding for the e-book with permission from the copyright holder.	On the face of it, this is a very useful feature for supporting literacy development; for example, as a pronunciation guide. However, it is limited and fully accessible features such as annotation and notes options are not usually available for text to speech. Text to speech on the Kindle Keyboard is not a very pleasant user experience. The voice is robotic and there are unsuitable pauses and many mispronunciations – not a

	Feature	Detail	Considerations and tips for use in the classroom or learning activities
	Built-in software functions		
15	**Text to speech (cont.)**	(Please refer to Chapter 3 for further information on DRM.) Text to speech is supported on the iPad and iPod on the iBooks app using the built-in VoiceOver accessibility function of the iPad/iPod itself. Some smartphones will have an in-built text reader or may support an app that reads text, although these may not work with all e-book reading apps.	voice you can listen to for very long. However, it does offer a choice of male or female voice and three speeds – both of which can be helpful to learners, as the features allow learners to choose the voice and speed that best suits their needs. The latest version of the Kindle Keyboard also includes an in-built Voice Guide that reads menu items, which is particularly important for visually impaired learners. To listen to a sample of some of the voices available with the Kindle, iPad and some other screen reader software, please visit the RNIB website page on e-book TTS: www.rnib.org.uk/livingwith sightloss/readingwriting/ ebooks/Pages/text_to_speech .aspx It's useful to note that if e-readers offer text to speech, then they will have speakers, and will also support audio files, which opens up many possibilities for learning (please refer to feature 13 in this table).

Feature	Detail	Considerations and tips for use in the classroom or learning activities
Built-in software functions		
16 **Text/ background colour and contrast options** Refer to the Newcastle City Learning case study and analysis in Chapter 4	With the e-ink screens, text is usually sharp and clear in greyscale with very little glare, akin to print (some now support colour too, such as Kobo Vox). E-readers with the greyscale e-ink screens don't have options to change the text or background colour; hybrid e-readers such as the Kobo Vox have limited options, such as sepia or night, whereas e-book apps used on the multifunctional e-reading devices have more options for text-contrast features; for example, the Kindle app on the iPad.	Consider these functions for learners where this is essential; for example, those with dyslexia or visual impairments (please refer to Chapter 3 for more information).
17 **Font size** Refer to the Treloar College case study and analysis in Chapter 5	All of the dedicated e-book readers have this function built in, the variation being in the number of text sizes available. For example, the Sony Reader provides eight sizes and the Kobo Touch provides 17 font sizes. Increasing the font size using this function does not affect the reflow of the text on e-books in e-book format (but beware, some e-books offered in .PDF format do not	Being able to change the font size to suit is one of the best features to meet the needs of all your learners, with particularly obvious benefits for learners with poor or partial sight; each learner can select the size of font that allows them to comfortably read the text. As this can be done discreetly, learners are more likely to continue reading wherever

Feature	Detail	Considerations and tips for use in the classroom or learning activities
Built-in software functions		
17 **Font size (cont.)**	accommodate reflow). Some touch e-readers also allow zoom magnification, such as Sony Reader, but this may mean that the text will not flow and the screen needs to be scrolled in order to read the text on the screen. Be aware that this functionality is generally only available for the text inside a book, and is therefore not available for annotations, menus or lists of books on the e-reader.	and whenever they want to, such as on the bus or train, as being seen with large print books can be discouraging, and so may limit their time with the book. Be aware that PDFs behave differently and some native PDFs may not accommodate font size changes unless converted to another format (if the coding allows). The zoom feature on some e-readers and e-book apps may enlarge the PDF and so magnify the text, but then the text does not reflow and requires scrolling to view the other parts of the document.
18 **Font style**	Most e-readers allow users to select a different font style, including at least one serif and one san serif. E-book reading apps on multifunctional devices generally have many more font style options.	A useful feature for those learners (for example, those with some form of dyslexia) who find the serif font merges letters, thus confusing word patterns, which is a reading strategy we all use when reading.
19 **Words per line and line spacing**	Available on some e-readers and most e-reading apps.	

Feature	Detail	Considerations and tips for use in the classroom or learning activities
Built-in software functions		
20 **Bookmarking** Refer to the South Staffordshire College case study and analysis in Chapter 5	A very useful feature for readers so you always come back to where you left off. It also synchronises with other devices or apps (registered on the same account) on which you are reading the same book. An option to go to the last read page is usually given when returning to the e-book.	Useful for group learning, where learners can read the same book and discuss aspects in class. If using a number of devices registered to the same account, with different learners reading the same e-book, the synchronisation feature can lead to confusion. However, it can be easily managed by switching the WiFi off and teaching your learners to choose the correct option when returning to their e-book. Switching the WiFi off prolongs the battery power.
21 **Highlighting and annotation** Refer to the 'ReKindling the Fire' case study and analysis in Chapter 4	Words, phrases and paragraphs can be highlighted and saved in lists with annotation – useful for coming back to later for reference or discussion.	For literacy learners, this function can be used in a variety of exercises for literacy skills development; for example: highlighting and annotating synonyms or metaphors; phrases that have a particular meaning; words or phrases used in different contexts, etc. These can be particularly useful for ESOL learners. Highlighting and annotation combined with the look-up dictionary feature (see feature 22) gives learners a

Feature	Detail	Considerations and tips for use in the classroom or learning activities
Built-in software functions		
Highlighting and annotation (cont.)		way of creating their own dictionary of unfamiliar words with explanations in their own words to help them learn.
22 **Look-up dictionary**	Most of the e-book readers (and e-book apps) offer this feature. It allows the reader to look up the meaning of an unfamiliar word whilst staying on the page, thereby not having to find or use a different tool like a dictionary or find someone to ask. Note: this feature may only be available for e-books from the e-reader's own store and not to those added from other stores. Features to look out for: 1) Ease of looking up definitions – for some e-readers, you need to locate the cursor by the word using the joystick or menu navigation buttons, which can be a little fiddly as they are so small and require accurate pressing. For the touch-screen e-readers, such as the Kindle Touch, you need to tap on the word for the dictionary definition to appear at the bottom of the screen; this	This is a useful feature for struggling literacy learners. Being able to immediately find out what an unfamiliar word means leads to less disruption in concentration and focus whilst reading. The availability of dictionaries in a variety of languages is a significant benefit for learners whose first language is not English – being able to understand the meaning of the word from the foreign language translation can help them understand and use the word when speaking or writing in English.

	Feature	Detail	Considerations and tips for use in the classroom or learning activities
	Built-in software functions		
22	**Look-up dictionary (cont.)**	also requires accuracy of movement, but is generally easier to manage. The Sony Reader includes a stylus to help manage this. 2) Type of dictionaries available – most have the English-to-English dictionaries and some have English to other languages such as French or Spanish.	
23	**Search the contents**	A search feature is available where you can find other instances of a particular word/phrase in the book. The new Kindle Touch is trialling an X-ray feature, invented by Amazon, which provides additional information, gathered from communities of readers, about interesting aspects of the book, such as the characters, historical figures, places or events. The downloaded e-book comes with an extra file containing the curated content.	This feature allows learners to understand how a word or phrase can be used in different contexts. Unlike with a printed book or magazine, you cannot physically browse an e-book's content by easily flicking through the pages, so the search feature can help learners find a place in the book about something they have already read and want to refer back to. Amazon's X-ray feature on the Kindle Touch is accessed by a single tap, which shows the 'bones of the book'. It can be used to help learners get deeper into the contexts and concepts in which the story is

	Feature	Detail	Considerations and tips for use in the classroom or learning activities
	Built-in software functions		
23	**Search the contents (cont.)**		wrapped up. This is very useful for differentiation when setting up a reading activity or exercise.
24	**Social networks/ communities**	Most e-readers and e-book apps include a feature (via Internet connection) allowing readers to discuss and share ideas about the e-book they are reading with others who may be reading the same e-book.	This feature can enhance the reading experience, but may also cause distractions. It also means that WiFi needs to be switched on which can drain the battery. Amazon's new X-ray feature uses the community discussions to provide extra associated background material in each e-book.
25	**Printing e-books**	E-books are usually not suitable for printing; often this is encoded in the DRM system used. Native PDFs can be printed.	While this might be useful for some, it is not advised, as there is generally no actual print option, so it can get a bit messy to do.

E -book apps

With the availability of e-book apps, you don't even need a dedicated e-reader. You can use an app on other multifunctional devices, such as tablets, computers and smartphones. There are many advantages for learners:

1   If they already have a device, and many learners now have smartphones or iPads, then they can access e-books without the need to buy a dedicated e-reader.
2   It avoids the need to carry more than one device, which is very popular with young learners.
3   Familiarity with the device through regular use and, if using a computer/laptop, own familiar input devices (keyboard and mouse).
4   Many of the apps can work with built-in screen readers and other accessibility strategies such as keyboard navigation.
5   Many more options for adjusting the text style, size and background for a more comfortable reading experience for all learners. (Please refer to *Chapter 3* on access and accessibility for more details).
6   Includes the useful functions that are also available on the e-readers such as the look-up dictionary, highlighting and annotation.
7   Most devices will run more than one app, allowing you to read books from different e-book stores and libraries all on the same device.
8   The devices support colour, which makes reading more appealing.
9   The devices support multimedia, such as audio and video, so can run e-books where these are used in the creation (refer to the GABES case study in *Chapter 4* for more information). For example, the Beatles *Yellow Submarine* e-book read in iBooks on the iPad has video clips throughout to further illustrate the story, making it come alive.

10 Tablets and computers, with larger screens, are more comfortable for reading magazines and e-newspapers, and navigation is much easier using either the touchscreens or keyboard and mouse – also, they support colour. Smartphones and iPods can be used for e-magazines and e-newspapers, but are not such a good user experience as the screens are smaller. Dedicated e-readers can also be used, but have the same disadvantage of the small screen and don't support colour. This is where the hybrid e-readers such as the Kobo Vox are attempting to strike a balance between the portability and readability and additional functions.

Example of a magazine displayed on a larger screen

If learners have access to a dedicated e-reader such as a Kindle, Kobo or Sony Reader and a multifunctional device, such as a smartphone, they can read e-books or other handouts and documents on either by installing the associated app on the device. By registering both the e-reader and the app to the same account, they can synchronise and open the book they are currently reading at the place they left off on whichever device they are using at the time.

All the major e-book stores offer their e-book apps free of charge and on the following page we review just a few types to give you a flavour of what's available.

App	Detail	More information
Adobe Digital Editions	Supports .EPUB format e-books and PDFs. Required for DRM-protected Adobe PDFs and .EPUB format e-books borrowed from libraries.	http://www.adobe.com/products/digitaleditions
Calibre	This is a multifunctional app that not only allows you to read books but also convert books from many formats into many other formats – very useful for creating e-books from your own documents (please refer to the section on 'Creating your own e-books' in Chapter 7).	http://calibre-ebook.com/about http://calibre-ebook.com/download
iBooks	This is an Apple app for use on Apple devices such as the iPad and iPod. The advantage of this is that it works with the built-in VoiceOver function installed on the device which reads the text (refer to the GABES case study in Chapter 4).	http://www.apple.com/support/ios/ibooks
Kindle	For Kindle books in the .AZW format and PDFs.	http://amzn.to/kindleappsforebookdevices
Kindle for PC with accessibility plug-in	This has been designated assistive technology software rather than an e-book app. The advantage is that the built-in voice engine will read all Kindle books, even if this feature has been disabled in the e-book (please refer to Chapter 3 on access and accessibility for more information on this app.).	http://www.amazon.com/gp/feature.html?ie=UTF8&docId=1000632481
Reader for PC/Kobo	For .EPUB format e-books and PDFs.	http://ebookstore.sony.com/download http://www.kobobooks.com/smartphones

App	Detail	More information
Stanza	Available for use on Apple devices and available only from the iTunes store. It has great accessibility features, such as being able to change the colour of the text and background. It also works with the VoiceOver function of the Apple device.	http://itunes.apple.com/gb/app/stanza/id284956128?mt=8

CHAPTER 3
Access and accessibility

E-readers and e-books are a boon for learners who have visual difficulty reading print or have physical or motor disabilities which make printed books hard or heavy to hold and pages tricky to turn, as these digital technologies can mean better or greater access to text. (Please see *Chapter 4* for case study examples.)

For example, with publishers beginning to launch books in physical *and* digital formats together, blind or partially sighted readers can now enjoy those books at the same time as everyone else, although there's still a long way to go before the majority of books are produced as e-books as well. Conversely, due to the ease and reduced costs of producing and publishing e-books, some books are being published in this format only which, again, may mean some learners who cannot use the digital versions lose out.

E-book format

Digital files that are referred to as e-books can be created in different formats designed to be:

▶ read using an e-reader or e-book app on a multifunctional device such as a computer, tablet or smartphone. These look like a book, with pages that are 'turned' to simulate reading a book and a contents page. The formats for these are the proprietary format such as Amazon's .AZW, which can be read on Amazon's e-readers (Kindles) only or the open standards format, such as .EPUB, or .PDF; or

▶ read in web browsers on a tablet or computer, with similar features as above. The formats for these are generally versions of

.HTML or .SWF formats. Some hybrid devices such as the Kobo Vox and some smartphones with good web browsers may also support these e-books, but will quickly drain the battery as they require a lot of processing power. Examples of these can be found at:

Staffs PDC Moodle – English and Mathematics Qualifications at Level 2:

www.staffspdc.org.uk/pluginfile.php/4108/mod_resource/ content/6/English_and_Mathematics_e-book/ebook/index.html; or

Solihull College prospectus: www.typmagazine.co.uk

Some browser-based applications that read e-books in .EPUB formats are also available, such as the IBIS Reader[4] or Project Gutenburg.[5]

TIP!

WebbIE is a set of free software programmes developed by Alasdair King[6] for blind or partially sighted people. As well as being an accessible web browser that works with own-installed screen readers such as JAWS or Thunder (discussed later in this chapter) and other useful software, the set includes a Gutenburg Library plug-in.

Digital rights management (DRM)

E-books can be created in open or restricted format decided by the copyright holder. Copies of open format e-books, usually in the .EPUB and .PDF file formats, can be transferred between devices that support these formats, such as the Sony and Kobo e-readers.

4. Available at: http://ibisreader.com
5. Available at: www.gutenberg.org/catalog/world/readfile?fk_files=1529528
6. Available at: www.webbie.org.uk/about.htm

However, all digital content (video, music or e-books) can be encoded using a digital rights management (DRM) system to control access, copying and distribution of the content in order to protect the rights of the author/creator, publisher and distributor. Specific DRM systems are developed by specific companies, such as Apple and Adobe, with different layers of protection or restriction. DRM-restricted e-books will require the reader to agree and comply with the terms of the encoded restrictions. For example, Adobe DRM requires the reader to initially create a personal ID with Adobe® Digital Editions – ADE). Then each device the reader intends to use to read Adobe DRM-restricted e-books must be authorised with ADE using the personal ID.

'Authorise Computer' in ADE Library options

Confirmation of authorisation returned

Library e-books often use the Adobe DRM system and they are encoded for short-term lending. In the same way as the number of physical copies that a library has available for lending at any one time, e-books are encoded for the number of copies that can be made available to lend out at the same time and the duration for which each copy can be borrowed. Once the duration has expired, the e-book digital file is scrambled so the reader can no longer read it. In effect it 'comes back' to the library, allowing the library to lend the e-book to someone else. To read the library e-book, borrowers can use Adobe's own e-book app, Adobe Digital Editions, or another app (such as Bluefire) or device (such as Sony Reader) which supports the Adobe e-book format. However, the reader must authorise each app or device that they intend to use to read the library e-book with Adobe.

DRM restrictions placed on e-books can have major implications for learners and learning providers. For example, copyright holders authorise how many devices (usually registered to the same account) the book can be made available on. They can also decide to encode the e-book so they can or cannot be 'lent' to someone else by electronically sending the book to their device. Other accessibility functionality can also be restricted through DRM, such as 'text to speech' (TTS).

E-book stores will often state if specific books are DRM-free, so it's worth looking out for this designation, as it will mean more flexibility for you and better accessibility for your learners.

Example of an e-book store homepage

TIP!

Using e-books in the classroom and in college libraries is still fairly new and the conventions surrounding the use of e-books are still being developed, so when in doubt always check with your own organisation, who may then want to take further advice.

Text to speech (TTS)

Text to speech, or TTS, is a feature that can really help make written text more accessible for learners with visual impairments. Unfortunately, not all e-books are enabled to allow this feature and not all e-readers include this feature.

E-readers

Only a few e-readers offer this facility, e.g. Amazon's Kindle Keyboard and Kobo Vox. Be aware, though, that there are limitations on which parts of the e-reader screen and e-book is available to the TTS software. Mostly TTS will read only the body text of an e-book, and menus and navigation help such as contents pages and indexes are not available to the TTS software.

E-book apps

On other devices, built-in TTS software or applications can provide TTS capability, such as the VoiceOver function on Apple's iPad with the iBook app. (Note that it doesn't work with other e-book reading apps installed on the iPad.)

Screen readers, such as Thunder[7] or JAWS,[8] installed on computers, will read e-books in the .HTML format that opens in a web browser, making this format highly accessible to learners with visual impairments or learners with dyslexia where hearing the text supports reading.

Screen readers will work with some window and menu titles of e-book apps, such as the Kobo or Adobe Digital Editions; however, the book text is usually not available to the screen readers.

---

7. See www.screenreader.net for information on the Thunder Screen Reader and a free download of the software; also available in other languages.
8. JAWS Screen Reader is available for download from different sites – please use a search engine to find the sites.

The Kindle for PC with accessibility plug-in app is, currently, the only app that can read text, even where the TTS feature has been locked out by DRM. This provides a number of features:

▶ TTS reading with adjustable voice settings;

▶ voice-guided menu navigation;

▶ large font sizes;

▶ high contrast reading mode;

▶ keyboard navigation; and

▶ accessible shortcuts.[9]

Voice-guided menu navigation works with a screen reader installed on your own computer, such as those referred to above. The body text is read by a voice engine built into the app and activated by a shortcut, allowing you to control when the text is read. As this is considered to be accessibility software it works with Kindle books, even where the text to speech has been disabled in the DRM coding.

Text size, type and layout
The ability to change text size and style to suit the learner is generally available on all e-readers and apps to varying degrees (for e-readers, refer to the e-readers and devices features table in the *Appendix*).

Reflow
One of the really important features to look out for in e-books is flowability when increasing font size – do the lines wrap and flow on the screen? This is very much dependent on how it was created and what features are enabled. E-book formats such as .EPUB, .AMZ and .MOBI generally allow reflow. Some e-books in the .PDF format will allow reflow, whereas others are sometimes locked down to maintain the original layout and content just as it was created, so

---

9. Information on this can be found from:
www.amazon.com/gp/feature.html?ie=UTF8&docId=1000632481

lines of text may not flow if the font size or magnification is increased – you need to use the scroll bars to see all the text. Some PDFs will convert to an e-book format such as .EPUB to allow reflow.

Number of words per line and line spacing

These can be beneficial features for learners with dyslexia or cognitive disorders, as well as to help with literacy development in low-level learners. To be able to adjust the words per line can help avoid overwhelming the learner with a large volume of text to read and leaving white space between lines helps in clearly defining lines and text.

E-book readers

All versions of the Kindle offer both of these features. Some of the other devices offer the function of adjusting margin size, which can adjust the number of words per line, but does not change the line spacing.

E-book apps

The Kindle app has a slider to control the number of words per line, i.e. the number of words that appear on the screen at any one time. The Kobo app has a slider to control the margin width; used together with the font size slider control, the number of words on screen can be adjusted.

Some apps also allow options for changing line spacing.

Text/background colour contrasts and options

Many learners find the default text colours of black on white stark and uncomfortable for reading. Learners with a specific type of dyslexia, for example, prefer a different colour contrast to enable them to better access text.

E-book readers

The dedicated e-readers specialise in the grey-scale e-ink displays and usually have no options for changing this as colour is not supported. The hybrid e-readers have limited options; for example, Kobo Vox has a sepia and night option with brightness adjustment.

E-book apps

E-book reading apps used on multifunctional devices generally offer at least three modes: white, sepia and black (see below for examples). This is particularly useful on these devices as the screens on the multifunctional devices are not glare-free and can be tiring on the eyes.

The Stanza e-book reading app, available for Apple devices, is one of the best apps, with a wide selection of text colour and background colour.

Weight

Dedicated e-readers are lightweight and easier to hold, even in one hand, for a useful period of time for reading a book, making these devices a good choice for learners with some physical difficulties who find physical books too heavy to hold.

Support organisations

AbilityNet has produced a factsheet with guidance on electronic publications for learners:
www.abilitynet.org.uk/factsheet/electronic-publications-0

JISC TechDis is working with publishers and the Right to Read Alliance to maximise the potential of e-books and e-readers for disabled learners:
www.jisctechdis.ac.uk/techdis/technologymatters/beyondtext/differentformats/ebooks

The **RNIB** (Royal National Institute for the Blind) is very interested and active in the developments in the digital books industry, as the organisation wants to ensure the needs of people with visual impairments are considered when e-books are made available:
www.rnib.org.uk/professionals/accessibleinformation/electronicdocuments/ebooks/Pages/ebooks.aspx

CHAPTER 4
E-readers and e-books in use

Examples of use in learning

The following pieces of research and case studies demonstrate how e-books and e-reading devices have been used in learning over the last couple of years. There are examples from compulsory and further education, as well as from a number of different countries. They have all been published elsewhere and details of how to access the full reports are at the end of each study.

 Dudley College: Stimulating the use of mobile technologies in work-based learning (2010)

JISC Regional Support Centre West Midlands devised a project, 'The Learning Journey Made Mobile,' to explore the use of mobile technologies to potentially enhance aspects of the learner journey. One of the organisations that took part in this project was Dudley College, which wanted to use Amazon Kindles to supply course-related materials and college policies and newsletters to workplace learners.

Impact

- Learners tended to use the Kindles more for reading fiction.
- Locating relevant curriculum resources was difficult.
- Sometimes a Kindle download is cheaper than the physical book.
- Purchasing e-books was very easy.
- Documents can be delivered to the Kindle via a USB cable connected to a computer.
- Learners could easily delete or move around books into different folders – this could be problematic.

Advantages and disadvantages

Advantages	Disadvantages
Good size	Reading in low light is difficult
Lightweight	Needs a colour touch screen
Possible to make notes	Navigation using the buttons, especially on the Internet, is challenging
Battery life is very good	You don't get the feel of a book when using a Kindle
Possible to access the Internet	Resources not quite right for the course selected for the trial
Possible to change the text size on screen	Using the small buttons and keypad was difficult
The book can 'read aloud' to you	
Screen orientation can be changed	
Content can be organised into folders	
The screen is clever as it does look like paper and reduces eye strain, unlike other devices	

The college staff who evaluated these devices don't think that they will be using the Kindles in a work-based learning setting again, primarily due to the lack of resources available during the pilot stage. However, they noted that they may be able to use them in a library setting to encourage reluctant readers to adopt the new format to help develop their skills.

To access the original report, go to:
http://wiki.rscwmsystems.org.uk/index.php/Learning_Journey_Made_Mobile
Reproduced with kind permission from JISC Support Centre West Midlands and Dudley College
© *JISC Regional Support Centre West Midlands*

Newcastle City Learning: Using e-readers with adult literacy learners (2011)

As part of a JISC Regional Support Centre (RSC) Northern action research project, Newcastle City Learning received six Kindle e-readers to trial with three identified groups of Skills for Life (SfL) learners. The aim of the project was to investigate the effectiveness of e-book readers for SfL learners, including dyslexic and visually impaired learners. Paul Miller at JISC RSC Northern provided Newcastle City Learning with six Kindles which were pre-loaded with 16 'Quick Reads' e-books, selected by the SfL team (the SfL co-ordinator Anna Brown and two tutors – Judith Rust and Cathy Stark). After the acquisition of the e-books, the Kindles were de-registered before they were issued to the learners to prevent unauthorised purchases.

Advantages and disadvantages

Advantages	Disadvantages
More comfortable reading from a Kindle because nobody else could see what they were reading. One learner commented: 'You could be learning to read or reading *War and Peace*. If you're learning to read you could disguise it with a Kindle.'	Synthesised speech has a USA accent and a lack of intonation or emotion. Expensive to purchase.
The devices are small and light, which assists learners with physical disabilities like arthritis.	Colour couldn't be changed for learners with dyslexia.
Increasing font size and spacing helped, especially those with dyslexia or visual impairment. One learner said: 'I like the fact that the Kindle screen has an anti-glare element to it and you can change the font size.'	No touch screen; the buttons are rather small and fiddly. Have to re-register then de-register for more purchases.
Variable speed voice function assisted learners with pronunciation and to read along.	
On-demand dictionary particularly useful for learners whose first language was not English.	
Learners felt motivated to read from a Kindle because the technology was 'cool'.	

The impact and lessons learned
The Kindles have encouraged some learners to read more and have helped to develop their skills with digital technology. The Kindles are in constant use in the SfL provision at Newcastle City Learning, and a significant number of learners stated that, when offered the choice, they preferred to read from the Kindles. The SfL team would have liked more books for the Adult Core Curriculum/Functional Skills to be available for Kindles. They contacted various publishers about this issue and, as a result, Readwell Road publishers agreed to a trial with Newcastle City Learning to make their series of structured reading books for adult learners available in e-book format.*

To find out more and to watch a video about this case study, go to:
http://www.excellencegateway.org.uk/node/20459
Reproduced by kind permission of Paul Miller at JISC Regional Support Centre Northern
© JISC Regional Support Centre Northern

> *While Readwell Road did agree to produce its books in an e-book format, the company is a small business and has encountered some difficulties around DRM and copyright issues. Once these issues are resolved, they should be able to offer e-books.*
> *Go to www.readwellroad.com for more information.*

CASE STUDY

ReKindling the fire: Using Kindles for literacy in the classroom (2010)

Faye Bormann and Kaye Lowe undertook research in the Australian classroom entitled: *ReKindling the Fire: Using Kindles for literacy in the classroom*. They worked with reluctant readers and writers, and found that literacy learning outcomes were improved by the use of e-readers.

Access and flexibility
The Kindle opens up the world of books and reading material such as e-newspapers, and some of the classics which are now out of print can be downloaded free from Amazon. The reader can place the cursor before an unknown word and the dictionary meaning

will appear at the bottom of the page. The search function on the Kindle allows readers to search for words, phrases and character names in the book.

Text to speech
Where the author permits, the text-to-speech facility enables the reader to listen to the text being read. The pages turn automatically, leaving the hands free. Male or female voices can be chosen and the speed of reading can be adjusted according to the reader's needs.

Readability
The Kindle has a paper-like display with black ink which reads just like real paper without the glare of a computer screen. It is easy to read in full sunlight. Readers stated that they liked the largest font because it was clear, made them less tired and helped them to read faster.

Seamless reading
Page turning on the Kindle is designed to be effortless, becoming more of an unconscious movement of the thumb to allow the reader to disappear into the story.

Guided/group reading
E-readers can provide an engaging way to work in small groups for guided reading. Learners can highlight particular words in the text using the highlight function. Word meanings are instantly displayed at the bottom of the screen once the cursor is placed before the word. The note-taking function allows learners to write and store their opinions or questions. When discussing particular words learners can type the word in the search feature and all the places in the text where this word appears are listed. Bookmarking is useful if the student is using the same Kindle each time. If not, they can record the number of the last location read and easily return to their place in a subsequent session.

Motivating writers

Many learners are keen to read but can be more reluctant when it comes to writing. This can occur for many reasons, the most common being a fear of being unable to spell words. The possibility of publishing on a Kindle can be enticing. Writing can be published on a computer, and illustrations scanned in and then saved onto the Kindle as a PDF file.

Taken from the full article on this project: Faye Bormann and Kaye Lowe (2010) 'ReKindling the Fire: Using Kindles for Literacy in the Classroom', in 'Literacy Learning: Middle Years Journal', Vol. 18, October 2010.
Reprinted here by kind permission of the Australian Literacy Educators' Association: www.alea.edu.au
© Australian Literacy Educators' Association

CASE STUDY | **Using electronic books in the classroom to enhance emergent literacy skills (2010)**

In 2010, Amelia Moody published an article in the *Journal of Literacy and Technology* entitled: 'Using electronic books in the classroom to enhance emergent literacy skills'. She has researched the use of e-books in the classroom and has distilled down her findings into a best practice guide.

Moody highlighted two areas where e-books can be particularly useful: reading engagement and scaffolding for emergent literacy development. Reading engagement refers to the ability of a student to sustain attention over time. Studies have shown that, compared to reading with the teacher, learners followed a text better when reading alone with the e-book. Similarly, the scaffolding meant that children using the interactivity of an e-book felt that they could read more independently, access dictionaries, hear words spoken and gain more comprehension than when being assisted by a teacher. There were also endless possibilities to read and re-read the digital text rather than having to wait for the teacher to be free to help the child.

Moody also found case studies where e-books had not shown better results than print books, but, significantly, they were no worse. According to Moody, one thing that has to be taken into question when using e-books in the classroom is if it is right for the student, and also whether the content of the e-book is appropriate for the student. One surprising finding was that some interactive features that are irrelevant to the text and the story can be distracting and can decrease the comprehension of the story. Also, rules need to apply in the classroom for e-book use: time expectations for completion; strategies for moving between pages; and interactional opportunities with peers.

Overall, Moody found that e-books could be very beneficial for learners who had difficulty learning to read, because it helped with reading engagement and, through scaffolding, helped comprehension, vocabulary development and phonological awareness in learners. However, care had to be taken to choose the right e-books, use traditional print books as well, mix independent reading with teacher supervision and monitor any distracting features embedded in e-books.

For more information on this study, go to:
http://literacyandtechnology.org/volume_11_4/JLT_V11_4_2_Moody.pdf
Reproduced by kind permission of Amelia Moody
First published in: Journal of Literacy and Technology, Volume 11, Number 4:
November 2010
ISSN: 1535-0975
©Journal of Literacy and Technology

GABES (Galway Adult Basic Education Service): The iPad in adult education (2011)

Galway Adult Basic Education Service (GABES) has successfully completed a pilot project which introduced iPads into the adult education classroom. Alison Jones, the iPad project coordinator, says that GABES is responding to the rapid development from *e*-learning to *m*-learning (mobile learning), and the need to equip adults with digital skills that will include and empower them in a world where those more technologically advanced are already using these devices for accessing information, buying and selling.

At GABES, each teacher devised a work scheme in which the integration of the iPad in the syllabus was clearly delineated. Pre-planning in this way avoids the random use of the iPad and deviation into its use as filler, as may happen with other 'devices'. Students learn the mechanics of usage first (for example, moving from screen to screen), and then build on what they may be comfortable with already, like looking things up online or using social media. In literacy classes, apps that develop spelling patterns, discourse patterns and document layout are used, whilst in ESOL (English for Speakers of Other Languages) teaching there are numerous apps available with typical grammar exercises. Popular English language books such as Raymond Murphy's *Practical English Usage* are also available in app form – which, of course, is more cost effective for students.

One of the most popular apps is 'Book Creator', where students can write their own stories and then save them to iBooks for other students to read. Tutors are also writing books as text books for use in class and as a means of presenting their students' work. The new audio feature in Book Creator has led to even more dynamic and lively books. iBooks allows students to read other books downloaded from the store, and also PDF documents which tutors can upload and use as classroom resources. The iPad has been especially useful for teaching spelling, with a variety of apps to choose from, including games such as Scrabble and Hangman and the newest addition: Chicktionary. Phonics, patterns and homophones are all catered for in numerous reading, writing and spelling apps. Numeracy classes have benefited from fraction apps, number squares and using the Penultimate app as a workbook.

Multiple apps (such as material on fractions and number recognition) are available for work in mathematics, whilst in special needs classes, different apps are used to enhance the functional independence of people with various types of learning disability. Ease of access is important for special needs classes – there is no need to operate a mouse or a switch, and there is even no need to sit a certain way, and built-in accessibility features such as zoom and high-contrast display also facilitate the visually impaired. The simplicity of programmes recommends it for special needs education, as does the availability of a protective case which makes it virtually indestructible.

Naturally there are limitations. iPads *are* initially expensive, but they are eventually cost-effective. They *are* open to technical failure, but so are computers and laptops. The overall outcome has been extremely positive. Students are eager to explore the new technology and find the iPad easy and attractive to use. It is an intimate learning tool and the increased confidence among students has been marked. It has encouraged students from one particular group to use the iPad to set up a Twitter account and a blog via apps that give easy access. Students tell us that they feel 'valued' and that they can't believe how much they are learning.

To find out more about the GABES iPad project and to watch a video about this case study go to: www.gabes.ie/index.php?gb=31
Reproduced by kind permission of Alison Jones and Kieran Harrington
© Galway Adult Basic Education Service

CHAPTER 5

Our own action research

This chapter consists of both case studies commissioned by us (the authors) as part of writing this book, as well as projects from learning providers who we had heard were currently using e-books in one form or another, and who have kindly allowed us to write up their findings. Whichever is the case, we would like to thank all of the people involved with these case studies for their time and expertise. Hopefully as you read through them they may inspire ideas for your own use of e-readers in the classroom. None of these case studies have previously been published.

CASE STUDY

**Nudrat Ali,
Joseph Chamberlain College
Family-friendly reading on
the PC
(2011–2012)**

Nudrat Ali is a literacy and ESOL teacher at Joseph Chamberlain College in Birmingham. She teaches out in the community and mainly teaches women who have English as a second or additional language. Nudrat decided to use e-books to be read on a web browser with one of her Entry 1 classes, who meet at St Paul's Community Foundation School in Balsall Heath, near to the college. The room that she teaches in has multiple PCs in it with an Internet connection. Nudrat's seven learners accessed free e-books from three websites:

- **Oxford Owl**: www.oxfordowl.co.uk/reading – this is a free site for parents to help their children with their reading.

- **Google books**: http://books.google.co.uk – Google has a mixture of free and paid-for e-books, which can be read on your PC or downloaded to an e-reader.

- **Obooko**: www.obooko.com – Obooko is a free e-book website; the books are mainly from new writers who want to self-publish. Registration is free.

Nudrat wanted to increase the learners' reading and understanding at sentence level. She also wanted to introduce reading for pleasure to a group of learners who tend not to read for pleasure in their own language. Nudrat was also keen to bring in an element of family learning to encourage the learners who had younger children to use the appropriate e-books with their children at home. Nudrat first introduced the learners to the concept of e-books and guided the learners in their use of the e-books as a whole group activity. Then she allowed them to work independently or in pairs (depending how confident the learners felt). The learners would spend half an hour at a time choosing a book, reading and showing understanding of what they had read. All of the learners were encouraged to try reading the e-books at home; they then reported back to the class about what they had read.

Benefits

The learners were excited by the use of the e-books and felt more independent in the classroom, which increased their self-esteem. The learners enjoyed using a 'new technology', and from Nudrat's point of view it is also another easy-to-access resource that adds variety. Once they became more confident, the learners enjoyed choosing their own books to read. Using the e-books has created a more positive approach towards reading. All of the learners accessed e-books at home, when they would often not use the computer at home at all. Learners could also use these stories with their own children if they wished to. Websites like Oxford Owls were particularly popular because text to speech could be used, and the stories were illustrated to aid understanding of the text.

Disadvantages

Nudrat found it was time consuming to find books that were at the right level for the learners, and they did find the reading and understanding challenging at first. Other than children's websites, it is difficult to find appropriate books for Entry 1 ESOL learners. Nudrat has assimilated e-books into her normal classroom practice, but feels that with higher-level learners they could be used even more. Having to register each learner to some websites and manage password control can be a bit of a problem. Although dictionary functions on some of the e-books are great, Entry 1 learners can struggle to understand the definition given by the dictionary.

Nudrat felt that the learners were interested and excited by the use of the e-books and the idea of reading; however, she does feel that more e-books need to be created with lower-level adult learners in mind, otherwise they need to rely on age-inappropriate books. A further feature could be a facility to highlight just one word within the text and hear that read aloud for pronunciation. She also felt simple dictionary definitions would be really worthwhile to match the level of reading.

TIP!

Although it is not within the text itself when reading, learners could use the website www.howjsay.com – an online dictionary which says the words in its dictionary out loud.

CASE STUDY

**Moira Johnson,
Treloar College
Bouncing books
(2011 onwards)**

Treloar College is an independent specialist college in Hampshire and offers residential and day provision for learners aged 16 to 25 with physical and sensory disabilities and/or other learning difficulties. Moira Johnson is the Learning Resource Manager and has kindly agreed to share the experience that the college has had with e-readers both in the classroom and the Learning Resource Centre.

Firstly, Moira would like to point out that it isn't a matter of deciding to use e-readers at her college, it is more a matter of looking at each individual learner and deciding what kind of equipment will help that particular learner, and in that way Treloar College has been using e-readers, in one form or another, for a number of years. The list of devices they have used to read e-books on includes:

- PCs;
- iPads;
- Kindles;
- smartphones using Android operating systems;
- tablets using Android operating systems;
- Apple smartphones (using IOS);
- Humanware Classmate e-book reader; and
- devices to access printed text, such as Intel Reader (portable and mounted options), Humanware My Reader and Humanware ScannaReader.

Treloar College has learners with various physical and learning disabilities and difficulties, so the staff encourage them to use any device and any format – whichever suits them. This makes it very difficult for Moira to say which device is better than another, purely because it is down to individual need. One thing that is recommended is that chunky cases are purchased for breakable devices, so when they are dropped, as inevitably they will be, not too much damage can be done. This is very important at Treloar College as many of the learners have poor motor skills.

The kinds of e-book that learners may read, include:

- e-books from e-book publishers and aggregators, such as Amazon;
- e-books-shared network locations; for example, Rising Stars Books[10] held in hard copy and in PDF versions for reading on a variety of e-reading platforms;
- e-books downloaded from Overdrive[11] – a portal for accessing e-books from public libraries; and
- freely available texts on the Internet.

Other than the Humanware Classmate e-reader, the college's own devices are not lent out to the learners; they are used within the confines of the Learning Resource Centre or in the classrooms. This is for a number of reasons, mainly concerned with keeping the devices in one piece and also because many of the learners lack mobility and motor skills, and would need someone around to help them access the devices.

The best feature on e-readers for Treloar's learners seems to be the ability to change font and font size to help the learners with visual impairments. The text-to-speech feature can be very useful, but only if it is a 'real voice'; the robotic voices can be very off-putting and do not help with pronunciation. Moira and her team have been heavily involved with the Six Book Challenge (see the next page for details) and are trying to encourage reading for pleasure with all readers from entry level upwards in the Learning Resource Centre and in the classroom.

10 www.risingstars-uk.com/categories/lit
11 www.overdrive.com

Moira feels that the e-readers can be a real help with independent reading, but she just wished that they bounced a bit more!

The Six Book Challenge is an annual incentive scheme with proven impact on literacy skills and reading motivation, and is now attracting 20,000 participants. For case studies, partnership models and guidance for public libraries, adult education, colleges, prisons and workplaces, go to: www.sixbookchallenge.org.uk

CASE STUDY

Alison Lathbury, South Staffordshire College E-readers as extension exercises (2012)

Alison teaches a variety of learners at South Staffordshire College with literacy skills roughly from Entry Level 3 to Level 2. She teaches Functional English and Maths as well as Skills for Life, so the age range of the learners is anything from 16 years of age and upwards. Alison has been evaluating a Sony e-reader and looking at how it could be used practically in her classroom situations. Alison has her own e-reader at home, which she uses frequently to read for pleasure. Before this case study she had not thought about using e-readers in the classroom.

> **"I would prefer to read something on my phone, rather than have to have an e-reader as well."**
>
> *Male learner, South Staffordshire College*

Once Alison had started to discuss using e-readers in the classroom with her learners, she was surprised to find that some of her adult learners already had e-readers and already used them for reading for pleasure. Many of her learners did not realise that there were features on their e-readers that they could use. For example, one of her learners, who had a Kindle, did not realise that there was a dictionary she could use as well.

Alison did a poll of her learners to see who would like to use an e-reader. The older learners were fairly positive, but the younger learners felt that the e-readers had been overtaken by tablets, which had many more uses. The Sony e-reader Alison was showing them in the classroom was one of the earlier models and the younger learners felt it was almost too old-fashioned, which made her worry about purchasing e-readers that very quickly seem out of date.

Alison had borrowed the Sony e-reader, so did not feel that she could give it to learners to take home, but it is in this area that she feels that e-readers could be of the greatest benefit. Alison does not have much spare time with her learners in the classroom, and has to get them through their examinations, which are literacy based rather than focused on literature. She feels that she does not have time in the classroom for extended periods of reading on the e-readers, so being able to lend out e-readers would be a great benefit. Learners may well go away from the lessons and read for pleasure more readily than if they were given a book. However, Alison does have large class sizes and feels that she would need a large number of e-readers to be able to exploit this.

From a value-for-money and function point of view, Alison would prefer to spend a budget on tablets rather than e-readers because they are more interactive and can be used in so many different ways. Alison feels that one way e-readers can still be used is by asking the learners if they have an e-reading device of some kind and encouraging the learners to download (free) content that is appropriate to them and will promote reading for pleasure and fluency. Perhaps the learners could all be encouraged to download the same book and read it away from the class so they can discuss it as a group in class. (If a learner does not have any kind of e-reading device, they could perhaps access the e-book on a computer at home or in the library, if possible.)

Alison is positive about the benefits of e-readers and how they can make reading for pleasure a more attractive and accessible option for learners, but feels that in large, one-hour Functional English classes they may be hard to use. However, using them as a way of encouraging independent reading and group reading away from the classroom could be a great solution. She feels that teachers should be aware of e-readers and how they work, so they can help learners to get the best from their devices and use them as extension exercises away from the classroom.

TIP!

Check out websites such as www.booksinmyphone.com/index.php that format and package free books to be read easily on Java-enabled phones.

Julie Wilkinson, Burton-on-Trent College Kindling a love of Shakespeare? (2012)

Julie Wilkinson is a Functional Skills teacher at Burton-on-Trent College in Staffordshire. She had one e-reader (a Kindle) to use with four vocational (catering) learners aged 16–25 who were taking Level 1 Functional English with Julie in the summer of 2012.

Julie downloaded a free copy of Romeo and Juliet onto the Kindle because her learners had expressed a desire to know a bit more about Shakespeare. Julie had paperback copies of the play and her teacher's copy had a modern translation alongside the original text, with cartoons of the action. Her primary learning outcome, as well as trying to increase their interest in reading for pleasure, was reading for meaning at sentence level. The learners also made great use of the e-dictionary. They used the e-dictionary in two ways: by just looking up a word to find its meaning, but also by being given words verbally that they had to try to define and to guess the spelling, using various strategies to help them look up the word in the dictionary to then confirm meaning and spelling. They also used the search function, which can help learners to understand meaning by finding a word used in different sentences.

Two of the learners in the class used the e-reader more than the others; this was a deliberate choice because one of the learners was partially sighted and the other was dyslexic. The learners only used the Kindle in the classroom, and were not allowed to take it home. This was because Julie had borrowed the e-reader. If it had belonged to the college, she would have encouraged the learners to use it outside of the classroom – although she would have de-registered the account first, so no books could be purchased 'accidently'.

Julie felt the most useful function on the e-reader was being able to change the size of the font. The partially sighted learner said that he liked being able to choose what size font he had each time he picked up the e-reader, as on some days he found he did not need as large a text size as on others. Having a built-in dictionary and search function was also invaluable. However, what Julie felt was lacking from a classroom point of view was the ability to change the colour of the background and the colour of the font – which would have been great for her dyslexic learner. Also, Julie was using the most basic Kindle with her learners, and she felt that spending the little extra money might be worth it for a touch screen.

Julie commented: *'I saw the learners, time after time, forgetting to turn the page by clicking a button and instead trying to swipe to the next page as they do with most of their touch-screen devices. Also, it seems that the click breaks the concentration slightly, whilst a swipe to the next page keeps the reading a seamless activity'.*

The learners did not use the text-to-speech function because the robotic voice detracted from the reading. However, Julie can see how useful text to speech would be if it was a 'real' person doing the reading or was more lifelike, but the robotic voice did not work in portraying Romeo wooing his Juliet. Julie felt that the e-reader made the work in the classroom seem more interesting to the learners, and they were happy to do work on the Kindle that they might not have done with a physical book and dictionary. The learners made the following comments:

- easier to read than a book;
- only need to tackle one page at a time – less intimidating than a book;
- would not want to be caught reading a book by friends, but happy to be caught reading a Kindle ('cool' factor);

- comfortable to read; and
- some of the learners now want an e-reader.

Julie had never used an e-reader before, so she took the Kindle home and played with it to make sure she felt comfortable using it with the learners. Julie, who reads for pleasure a great deal, was a little against e-readers as a general principle. She is now waiting for her birthday, when she hopes her family will have purchased a Kindle for her. She now supports the use of e-readers in the literacy classroom and also in educational libraries as a great way to encourage reading.

TIP!

Managing purchases: if you are buying Kindle devices and do not want the end users to be able to buy additional content, you can remove the method of payment from the Amazon account after any desired books are purchased. Alternatively, you can purchase Amazon.com Gift Cards and assign an Amazon.com Gift Card value to the account to limit purchases to a desired amount.

CASE STUDY

Thomas Bently, Stanmore College A wealth of e-books (2011 onwards)

Stanmore College, Middlesex, is a sixth form college that also delivers adult education and higher education provision. Thomas Bently, graduate trainee in the Learning Resource Centre, has kindly shared his research on buying e-readers for Stanmore College's library.

In 2011, the College purchased two Kindle e-readers, then later another two Kindles. The idea was that a learner could loan a

Kindle for up to two weeks at a time. The learner signs a borrowing agreement which also has a return date on it. The College then loads the book or books the learner has requested and the Kindle is de-registered and handed over to the learner. A charger does not need to be given out as the charge will last long enough for the length of the loan.

The library has not gone down the road of textbooks on the Kindle because there are so few textbooks that are available for the Kindle. Furthermore, the point of purchasing the Kindles was to encourage reading for pleasure. Stanmore College has been part of the Six Book Challenge (see the Treloar College case study earlier in this chapter for more information) and has found that people who would not normally have read a book for pleasure have been borrowing the Kindle to help complete this challenge. Over 50 per cent of the books the college has downloaded for the learners have been free books.

Thomas has said that the immediacy of downloading an e-book is such a boon in a library in a local college that cannot possibly always stock every book wanted by learners. He mentions a learner that came in and said that he wanted to look at Adam Smith's *An Inquiry into the Nature and Causes of the Wealth of Nations* for the course he was on; the library did not have a copy of the book, but within a couple of minutes a free copy of the book had been downloaded to the Kindle and handed over to the learner.

As well as immediacy, being able to change the font size is also a great advantage for learners who are partially sighted. Thomas thinks that the touch-screen option, which they do not have, would also be worth paying for because it helps with seamless reading and the learners seem to expect touch screens these days.

Thomas suggests that organisations who are going to buy a number of Kindles should buy Kindles in multiples of six. This is because any book purchased from the Amazon website can be put onto six devices as long as those devices are registered to the same account. Thomas feels that there is a lot of confusion around the lending out of e-books and their legal status for learning providers, because Amazon does not have a system for the distribution of e-books via libraries or for public use of any kind in the UK. JISC (a national body that supports technology in education and research) states the following:

> Lending Kindles preloaded with third-party content, such as an e-book currently in copyright, via a library or learning centre, would breach the current stated Kindle terms and conditions of use as far as UK users are concerned.

Thomas has approached Amazon directly and he has been assured that as long as books are not being shared between Amazon accounts then the books can be loaned to learners. More clarification is needed, but Amazon's stance is if you were to try to send an e-book registered in your name to a learner who has a Kindle registered in another name, then you would not be allowed to do that. However, it is possible to share content between six devices that are all registered to the same account and then share that content on the device with the learners. Thomas requests that organisations that have Kindles ask Amazon the same question, and hopefully the weight of opinion will make Amazon come out with definitive guidelines about the sharing of books (please refer to *Chapter 3* for more information about digital rights management and copyright).

Thomas is convinced that having the e-readers available for learners to borrow has meant that learners who would not normally borrow fiction books from a library have borrowed a Kindle and downloaded books to read for pleasure. He would like to encourage learners who do not have English as a first language to borrow the e-readers as well, but he has found that there are better traditional printed books appropriate for ESOL learners. He feels that there is still some way to go to make e-readers as effective as possible; for example:

- more e-books for ESOL readers are needed;
- clarification is needed around lending of content; and
- more textbooks need to be made available in e-book form.

Despite all of this, Thomas is looking to extend the number of e-readers they have in the library and feels that the project has been a complete success.

TIP!

Amazon offers a discount if you are making a bulk purchase of Kindles for an educational establishment (25 Kindles or more). For more information, visit:
www.amazon.co.uk/gp/help/customer/display.html/ref=cu_cfss_dyk_kindle_bized?nodeId=200627120

CHAPTER 6
Investing in e-readers and e-books

We intend this book and the information presented as a guide that we hope will help inform your decision:

▶ on whether e-readers and e-books are a worthwhile investment that will have real benefits for your learners; and

▶ if yes, what features will most benefit your learners, and which e-book reading device to invest in.

Throughout this book, there are suggestions and tips for use in the adult learning classroom. Technology is not straightforward to invest in. Much technology that grips the imagination of the learning provider has really been invented or developed with the private market in mind, but nonetheless has huge potential for learners and their learning.

As we have indicated, you may decide not to purchase any devices, but still want to exploit the potential of e-books for learners developing their literacy skills. This is entirely possible, and perhaps even advisable in some circumstances; for example, by using HTML e-books on your existing computers (please refer to the Joseph Chamberlain College case study in *Chapter 5*) or by installing e-book apps on your existing computers or using apps that run in web browsers, such as Ibis Reader.[12]

---

12. Available at: http://ibisreader.com

Hopefully, if you have been dipping into some of the chapters, you are ready to think about investing and what you need to consider to help make your decision.

Factors to consider

Staff needs

▶ Planning and scheduling training for staff and learners in using the devices and features to their potential is essential (please refer to the South Staffordshire College and Burton-on-Trent College case studies in *Chapter 5*).

▶ Access to a shared area for discussion is necessary and storage of resources that can be shared. Most organisations now run a virtual learning environment. Currently, Moodle[13] is the most popular in further education for teaching and learning. Special areas can easily be created for staff development and discussion on e-books/e-readers, as well as a repository for resources.

Learners' needs

▶ The profile of your learners that you intend to use the devices with, including:
  • technology awareness; individual interest and engagement with technology; and
  • current use and ownership of devices.

▶ Accessibility needs of learners who find it difficult to read print in traditional ways.

▶ Training needs on use of e-readers and e-books, including:
  • existing digital literacy skills; and
  • existing ownership and use.

(Please refer to *Chapter 3* for more information on access and accessibility.)

---

13. Moodle is an open source virtual learning environment and learner management system: https://moodle.org

Institutional considerations

▶ Cost of purchasing the devices and e-books. Consider mitigating costs by buying refurbished devices. Amazon sells refurbished Kindles and Apple sells refurbished iPads at reduced cost.

▶ E-readers and e-books are subject to VAT which can be reclaimed by VAT-registered businesses, thus reducing the final cost of purchase.

▶ Organisational systems that need to be put into place to help manage the use, storage and regular charging.

▶ Additional costs; for example:
  • chargers (not all devices come with chargers);
  • lockable cabinets, for storage with possibly built-in charging units;
  • device covers (and screen protectors if selecting multifunctional devices). Although durable covers can be expensive, we feel that they are worth the investment, as they aid the feeling of reading a printed book and also provide some measure of protection when in transit or being handled (please refer to the Treloar College case study in *Chapter 5*);
  • insurance is usually so expensive for education providers for these kind of devices that it is rarely worthwhile, but safety and responsibility is an issue; and
  • e-books. Whilst there are many hundreds of free e-books, consider if they are suitable for your learners; if not, factor in a budget (and system) for purchasing e-books.

▶ Guidelines and responsibilities for use with learners, including content purchasing, lending devices to learners (including in the event of loss or damage), and for learners to use their own devices, including smartphones.

Free e-books and e-book websites

Some teachers may worry that after purchasing e-readers they might not have an everlasting budget to buy many e-books. It is important to realise that it is perfectly legal to download free e-books. However, it is equally important to be able to spot something that is available as an illegal download, which constitutes piracy.

The three main reasons that an e-book may be free are as follows:

▷ The copyright has expired on a book, so it is in the public domain. Permission does not need to be granted for publication, and royalties do not have to be paid to an author. This is why so many of the 'classics' are usually available for free – because the author is no longer alive and copyright may have expired.

▷ Marketing reasons – an author/publisher may well be able to charge, but they decide not to – perhaps to raise the profile of the author and improve future sales.

▷ Some authors want their book given away for free to ensure a wider readership. Typically, this might be a charity, organisation or members of a religion who want to spread their e-word as far as possible.

TIP!

Many e-book websites offer the first chapter of a book free of charge to download, so the reader can see whether they like it before purchasing.

Websites for free e-books

The following are a few of the more major sites that offer free e-books.

Amazon	**www.amazon.co.uk**	Click on the Kindle department, and choose 'free e-book collections'
Free Tech Books	**www.freetechbooks.com**	Mainly for university-level learners and upwards
Google books	**http://books.google.co.uk**	Claims to be the first producer of free e-books
Internet Archive	**www.archive.org**	E-books and texts archive
Kobo	**www.kobo.com**	Offer books for sale as well as free e-books (click on 'free e-books')
Many Books	**www.manybooks.net**	Titles mainly taken from Project Gutenberg archives
Obooko	**www.obooko.com**	All free e-books are written mainly by first-time writers You can submit your own book for publication
Open Library	**www.openlibrary.org**	Part of the Internet Archive
Oxford Owl	**www.oxfordowl.co.uk**	Free books for children up to the age of 11 with audio, games and educational content
Planet e-book	**www.planetebook.com**	Classic literature
Project Gutenberg	**www.gutenberg.org**	Mixture of paid-for and free books
The Book Depository	**www.bookdepository.co.uk /free**	Sells e-books as well as offering them for free

Obtaining e-books for adult learners

"A beginner reader is not a beginner thinker."[14]

It is great that there are free books available for e-readers, but you might not find many of them appropriate for the level of reading that your learners are at. Even the children's classics (if you are happy to use them with adults) assume quite an advanced reading age; this effectively cuts out entry-level readers. Below we have provided a small list of publishers that offer e-books that are more suitable for adult learners.

Many (or possibly all) of the e-books available from the publishers that follow are books that have been written for paper format and have then been converted into an e-book – which might mean something as basic as a PDF file, or could even have just been provided on a CD-ROM to then be transferred to an e-reader. While this is better than nothing, it will be more interesting when books that have been specifically written for e-readers are made available, using some of the interactivity that is just waiting to be exploited. So, while we are asking publishers to provide adult literacy books in e-book format, we should also be asking the authors to think about writing adult literacy books for e-readers.

Quick Reads
Quick Reads are now available in e-book format (at the same price as the physical paper version).
www.quickreads.org.uk

Free chapters are available from the BBC Skillswise website.
www.bbc.co.uk/skillswise/learners/quick-reads

14. www.christinecoleman.net/early-influences-writing

Axis Education
All Axis Education books are now available as electronic books. Photocopiable titles are available as PDFs. If you want to read your book on an Amazon Kindle then you'll need a .MOBI file.
www.axiseducation.co.uk

Tribal
Tribal's online shop offers many of its literacy, language and numeracy resources as digital downloads, which can then be loaded onto e-readers.
https://shop.tribalgroup.co.uk

NIACE
Visit NIACE's e-bookshop to access e-books for and about adult learners.
www.niace.org.uk/publications/ebooks

ESL Publishing
This publishing house offers e-books with fully annotated footnotes, explanations of difficult words, phrases and expressions with an indication of the reading difficulty.
www.esl-publishing.com/products-page/ebooks

Gatehouse
Gatehouse currently publishes tutor resources as e-books (CD-ROM) and is looking to expand this area to respond to customer demand.
www.gatehousebooks.co.uk

TIP!

Remember to visit the 'Find a Read' website, which is provided by the Reading Agency and has an e-books section. It will show you what books are on offer and recommend books. Sudents can also recommend books for others to read:
www.readingagency.org.uk/findaread

Readability of e-books

Some websites for e-books give the 'reading ease' of a book in the details before you download the book. Often, the reading ease is given in the Flesch-Kincaid Reading ease score.

These scores can be interpreted as shown in the table below.

Score	Notes
90.0–100.0	Easily understood by an average 11-year-old learner
60.0–70.0	Easily understood by 13- to 15-year-old learners
0.0–30.0	Best understood by university graduates

Flesch-Kincaid Reading Ease Score[15]

15. http://en.wikipedia.org/wiki/Flesch%E2%80%93Kincaid_readability_test

CHAPTER 7
Suggested uses for the classroom

This section brings together some of the thoughts and ideas about using e-books in teaching and learning. The information has been distilled from published case studies, our commissioned case studies and discussions we have had with teachers as part of our research. We hope you find some of the ideas useful or that they will provide a jumping-off point for your own ideas.

As well as tools for developing reading skills, using the e-readers and multifunctional devices helps learners to become digitally literate, and removes barriers they may have in being able to access what they need to in modern, everyday life. Howard Rheingold, who has written widely on literacy and technology, believes that we need to think, not just in terms of 'literacy' but 'literacies' – to include digital, information and social media literacies.[16] Rheingold thinks that in different 'reading' situations we use different strategies, and our learners need to be helped with strategies for digital as well as paper reading.

Research is starting to show that reading on an e-reader slows your reading down a little (but is much improved compared with reading on a computer screen) and, because of the lack of visual cues you would normally get from a physical book, recall of what you have read is impaired slightly.[17] However, this research is being carried

---

16. www.educause.edu/ero/article/attention-and-other-21st-century-social-media-literacies
17. For more information, please see the following article: www.pcworld.com/article/200491/reading_on_paper_is_faster_than_ibooks_on_the_iPad.html

out on fluent readers who became fluent in reading in the traditional way. This may be the opportunity to develop students' skills to become fluent in both traditional and digital reading and to lay down new patterns of reading that work for our learners in a way that traditional methods have not. We firmly believe that e-readers are not just about substituting a physical book with a digital book; it is also about being given the opportunity to start to think about transforming the way learners undertake reading and tasks associated with reading, and transforming the way teachers think about using technology in the classroom.

Active listening: student is given text to listen to on an e-reader; the learner has to listen for specific information to be recalled or written down later.

Get learners to choose an article from an e-newspaper or e-magazine to use as a topic to discuss with the rest of the group.
Use e-newspapers to get different angles on the same story from around the world, to be able to discuss bias and language associated with objective and subjective articles – good for ESOL as well as literacy learners.
Use e-magazines to access information on hobbies to help learners to put together an oral presentation.

Discuss the different ways that learners approach reading a physical text compared to how they approach reading an e-book.

Speaking and listening

Learners with autism might prefer a robotic voice to help with reading and understanding, and if they use headphones it can cut out the other extraneous noises in the classroom that can prevent a student from concentrating on a text.

If there are technophiles and technophobes within a group, get those familiar with the devices to talk other learners through how to access e-readers. Learners could even come up with written, chronological instructions for future learners to follow.

Have a debate and a vote on who prefers e-books and who prefers physical books to read from and why. To promote the use of persuasive language, you could ask learners who prefer physical books to defend e-books and vice versa.

Pre-reading activity: to activate learners' prior knowledge before reading an e-text, have a discussion and get as many clues from the e-book as possible before reading it. This is also an easy way to become familiar with the functions and facilities an e-book can offer. This can also help to replace the cues that a physical book would provide.

How to choose an e-book
Work with learners on how to choose an e-book to read for pleasure and how to choose a physical book to read for pleasure. Discuss differences.

As a group project, the whole class could contribute pieces of work that are then uploaded to the e-reader in a magazine format.

In a family learning situation, learners could be encouraged to write their own books for their young children. This only needs to be a few pages with images and can include personalised information. They can then create their own e-book using free software such as Calibre to read with their children.

As a group project, the whole class could contribute pieces of work that are then uploaded to the e-reader in a magazine format.

Get learners to find five words in an e-article (related to them or their everyday lives) that they do not understand. Use online and conventional dictionaries to come up with a definition and share with other learners – this can be displayed on a wall or be kept as part of a personal dictionary.

Writing

For Functional Skills teachers, who are expected to know about different vocational areas to be able to embed Literacy, Language and Numeracy (LLN), downloading free magazines in those vocational areas can help to give ideas about how to exploit the LLN opportunities. They can also use the articles as part of exercises in the classroom.

In an ESOL class, learners could access e-newspapers from their own countries and use them as translation exercises in verbal and written formats. This would help learners from different areas of the world to understand a little more about each others' countries.

Learners could be encouraged to download an e-magazine about a hobby they are interested in and use that to wrap a topic around required learning outcomes.

Set up an e-newspaper or e-magazine treasure hunt where the student has to identify or find a select piece of information within the paper or magazine; helps with skimming and scanning and also helps learners to become very adept at using e-readers.

An e-reader can usually provide the following functions to exploit in the classroom:
- Text to speech – help with independent reading.
- Variable text size – to suit the needs of the student and the text.
- Built-in dictionary – seamlessly help to look up definitions without breaking the reading flow.
- Annotation and note taking – higher-level learners can take notes as they read to use in discussions and written work afterwards.
- Bookmarking – to be able to return to pieces of text or return to the furthest page read.
- Highlighting – highlight core parts of the text, or highlight words you don't understand.

Digital story-telling: learners tell their own story or share part of their everyday life with pictures and links to upload to an e-book to then share with others. This helps learners to understand the different way people live their lives and is great with a culturally diverse group.

When learners look up a word in an e-dictionary, get them to make a note of it, and see if they are able to spell the word; if not, develop a strategy to spell the word.

Take the Six Book Challenge: www.sixbookchallenge.org.uk or set up a reading group: http://readinggroups.org/tips/the-benefits-of-running-a-reading-group-for-adult-learners.html

Use e-newspapers and magazines to help to model the creation of your own e-newspaper or e-magazine to upload to an e-reading device.

Encourage diversity in what is read by accessing e-journals, e-magazines and e-newspapers from other countries as well. Many non-English-speaking countries produce an e-newspaper in English – such as the *Athens News* in Greece.

Visit authors' websites to find out about them, AND what else they have written. Get learners to e-mail favourite authors to suggest they write their next book in an e-book format.

Many organisations arrange a trip to the library to register to loan books and could then encourage learners to access e-books from the public library (if available). See Overdrive for participating libraries (www.overdrive.com).

Reading

Use e-newspapers and adverts in e-newspapers to help to teach audience and purpose of text.

Get learners to read a (free) chapter of a book and then, verbally or in written form, try to predict the way they feel the rest of the book might continue.

Teachers can send their own and already produced worksheets to the e-reader. This can be useful in community locations where there are no computers and can be used as extension exercises in a portable format.

For ESOL learners, ask learners to look in the e-text for:
- words with a particular suffix or prefix;
- compound words;
- words in the past, present and future tenses;
- possessives; and
- plurals.

Higher-level learners might look for examples of similes, metaphors, irony and hyperbole.

Set up an e-newspaper or magazine treasure hunt where the student has to identify or select a piece of information within the paper or magazine: helps with skimming and scanning and also helps learners to become very adept at using e-readers.

Family learning: learners can be encouraged to write e-books for children and read them to their children at home.

Create directed activities related to text (DARTs) to ensure that learners are reading and understanding e-texts. These can be paper based or uploaded to the e-reader.

ESOL learners can start by reading a text in their own language (if literate in own language) before they try one in English to help them feel comfortable using the device.

With thanks to:
Fouzia Tariq Choudhry – South Birmingham College
Helen Banks – South Staffs College
Louise Stirch – Learndirect (Pertemps)
Baljinder Bains – Burton College
Wendy Harrison – South Staffs College
for their help in coming up with ideas for using e-books in the classroom.

Creating your own e-books

Seeing their work in e-book format can be a fun and motivating activity for learners (see the 'Rekindling the Fire' case study and analysis in *Chapter 4)*. E-books can be created for an individual learner's writing or collectively as a group. Learners can write stories for an e-book to share with their children and friends (see the GABES case study and analysis in *Chapter 4*).

Whilst the RNIB guidance on producing e-books is aimed at the publishing industry, it may be helpful to read the document about issues to be aware of when creating e-books, particularly to ensure that accessibility is taken into account. More details and guidance can be found on the RNIB website:
www.rnib.org.uk/professionals/solutionsforbusiness/publishing/
Pages/publishing_industry.aspx

There are a number of free tools that allow you to create e-books.

Creating e-books from other documents, such as Microsoft Word or PDFs

Calibre for e-book management (available at www.calibre.com) is free, multifunctional software with several tools to help you manage your e-books.

The software needs to be installed on a computer and works offline. There is also a portable version which runs off a flash drive, so avoiding the need to install on a computer, which can be problematic in some organisations.

You can create e-books by converting a vast selection of digital files from one format into e-book format (and vice versa).

Amazon Self-Publishing Service

Amazon offers a service whereby e-books can be published using Kindle Direct Publishing and made available for sale to Amazon customers. This may be of interest to your learners (see the GABES case study in *Chapter 4*). More information, terms and conditions and responses to frequently asked questions (FAQs) about this service are available on Amazon's website:

www.amazon.co.uk/gp/help/customer/display.html?ie=UTF8&nodeId=200554840

Conclusion

> "It's not the changing nature of the book that scares me, but the unchanging nature of the reader – or rather our unchanging ways of educating readers."
> *Mark Craig (2011)* [18]

E-readers and multifunctional devices have great potential for adult learning. The obvious way to use them is simply as a substitute for a physical book. This has benefits, as the accessibility features are very helpful and so encourage reading, especially for struggling readers. However, we can seize this opportunity to help learners who have not yet laid down a pattern of reading physical books for pleasure to develop skills in navigating and enjoying e-books. As part of this, we need to transform some of the ways we think of interacting with books in our learning environments.

The popularity of the Internet has meant easy access to huge amounts of information. The Internet has changed the way we access information and, according to Nicholas Carr,[19] author of *The Shallows: What the Internet is Doing to Our Brains*,[20] how we read, think and remember.

For the majority of people, young and old alike, the Internet has become the first place to look for information, get news, go

---

18. Please see the full article that the quote is taken from here:
   www.marginlines.com/?s=nicholas+carr&searchsubmit=
19. Please see the full discussion with Nicolas Carr here:
   www.npr.org/templates/story/story.php?storyId=122026529
20. Carr, N. (2010) The Shallows: What the Internet is Doing to Our Brains. Norton & Co.

shopping, and communicate with friends and family. When reading on the Web, we wallow in the shallows (borrowing a phrase from Carr), moving quickly from one place to another space, gathering bits of information from different sources, at the same time juggling with a news story and communicating with friends on social networks, searching for prices of the thing you need or want to buy, and only sometimes going into depth on any one topic. With the advantages that technology can bring, e-books can bridge the gap between skimming content and plunging deeply when we want to. However, as with traditional methods, we must help our learners use the potential of e-readers and e-books to develop reading strategies to get the same, or perhaps even different, pleasures from reading.

Also, it is important to make use of the information-juggling habits learners are developing by structuring their flicking from one source to another to gather and build the blocks that will help them with their learning. If they are reading an e-book about life in Britain, which is useful for ESOL learners, why not direct them to go and find out more using the Web or get an answer to a question using Twitter? They can then annotate the e-book with their findings for future reference and reinforce their learning.

Research quoted in Carr's book shows that, left to themselves, learners are easily distracted by any number of things they find on the Internet, resulting in poor learning. However, by harnessing the richness of the Internet and other multimedia technologies in a focused way, learning can be scaffolded and differentiation catered for. Of course, there is the additional benefit of using technology in the classroom; that is, we should be helping our learners develop their digital literacy skills and using e-readers and e-books adds to that development.

Innovations in the e-reader market

We've highlighted some innovations here to give you a flavour of what to look out for now and in the future. The boundaries are blurring as developers try to provide a balance between the advantages of dedicated e-readers – portability through size and weight and readability through the innovative e-ink displays and long battery life – and the advantages of the multifunctional devices – web-browsing and being able to read in the dark.

Kindle solar case to extend battery life

The SolarFocus Solar Kindle case includes a light for reading in the dark which draws power from the solar charging panel built into the case and not the Kindle itself. The solar power can also add to the Kindle battery, so making it last even longer (three times longer according to the company). For more details, visit:
www.solarmio.com/en/4712389290366.aspx

Nook e-book glows in the dark

Barnes & Noble, USA-based retailer, has released a new version of its e-reader, the Nook, which glows in the dark, so there is no need for external lights for reading in the dark. The LED lighting system has been built into the e-reader frame which can be turned on for reading in low light. However, the Nook is only available in the USA and there is no indication whether it will ever be available for the UK market. For more details, visit:
www.bbc.co.uk/news/technology-17704009

Read your colour reader in bright light

Researchers at the University of Cincinnati are working on zero-power screens for smartphones and e-readers that support colour, so that videos can be seen clearly, even in bright light and without draining the battery quickly. For more details, visit:
www.smartplanet.com/blog/science-scope/new-color-e-reader-display-tech-promises-reading-in-direct-sunlight/4563?tag=btxcsim

High-speed ink system (HSIS)
The French company which retails the Bookeen e-reader has now released a version with HSIS. This provides a much faster refresh rate, so text refreshes quicker as you 'turn' the pages. It also provides a better browsing experience by having scrolling web pages, making it easier to pan around them. For more information visit: http://bookeen.com/en/cybook/odyssey

Innovations in the e-book market

First e-reader with native Google e-books integration
If your preferred e-book store is the Google e-books store, until now you will have had to download books on your computer and read them either on the computer's web browser or using the Google Play app on your multifunctional device, or transfer the file to an e-reader that supports Adobe's .ePDF format. Google has now released an e-reader, iriver Story HD, with direct access to the Google e-book store, much like the other e-readers reviewed in this guide, but currently only available in the USA. For more information, visit:

http://support.google.com/googleplay/bin/answer.py?hl=en&answer=179849

Bilbary lending library
Bilbary has a different e-book lending and selling model, based on agreements directly with the publisher, which will make the decision on whether to lend and/or sell. If publishers agree, patrons can choose to buy the e-book outright or rent an e-book for a short period. Currently, Bilbary has 2,500 publishers on board, including many of the big publishing houses such as HarperCollins, Simon & Schuster and Taylor & Francis. For more information, visit: https://uk.bilbary.com

Our thought piece

E-books and e-readers have been available for a while now. However, it has only been relatively recently that interest in both the format and device has soared, thanks in the main to Amazon for launching its first Kindle as a loss leader in 2007. As with other innovative technologies, educators will seize the opportunity for the benefit of learners, and as with other innovative technologies not specifically designed for education, e-books and e-readers have limitations for use with learners.

However, it is our opinion that the industry is still young and growing; manufacturers and publishers are still innovating and still keen to get a bigger slice of the market by listening to the loudest voices and developing their publications or devices to meet the demands. This is the time that we as learning facilitators need to make a noise about what we want from the industry.

The private reading market is being catered for, but they would be missing a trick if they didn't listen to the demands of learning providers – another huge market. The USA is way ahead with integrating textbooks into iPads and Google e-readers, but their market is different; their learning and teaching strategies are different. In the UK, we don't use standard textbooks across the sector; the adult education sector has developed to meet the needs of the individual learner and personalised learning is advocated by education policies.

There is therefore a need for much more flexibility in the technologies we might invest in for our learners. E-books and e-readers have been targeted in particular at the private market, but let's make a noise for the public sector now to inform and shape future development, while the manufacturers are still listening.

JISC TechDis has started the ball rolling over the last few years by, for example, working with the publishing industry towards accessible formats for e-books. It has also launched a website together with

the Publishers Association: Publisher Lookup UK
(www.publisherlookup.org.uk) for:

▶ educationalists seeking to source electronic formats of textbooks
for students with disabilities; and

▶ publishers seeking to respond in a timely and effective manner to
such requests.

Teachers involved in our own research (see *Chapter 5*) found that
more e-books suitable for adult learners engaged in literacy and
language development were needed. We need to lobby publishers
to make sure that they realise that there is a demand for e-books for
adult literacy and ESOL learners from Entry Level 1 upwards.

And finally...

...we would like to leave you with some work to do

Create your own materials
Teachers are resourceful, creative and imaginative, but are always
sorely pushed for time. So let's share the energy that is already
going into creating suitable e-resources for use with e-readers or
other multifunctional devices (for example see the GABES case
study in *Chapter 4*).

Contact the publishers
If you or your learners have favourite books or authors that you
would like to see published in an e-book format, then contact the
publisher and ask them if they have considered offering the book in
this format.

Contact the author
We do not just want to see paper versions of books converted into
e-books, we also want authors to think about how they could

exploit the interactivity of e-readers and multifunctional devices by writing e-books. So, get your learners to e-mail favourite authors and ask them if they have thought about writing an e-book.

Contact the manufacturers of e-readers

If you feel that there are functions and features that could usefully be added to e-readers, then contact the manufacturers to tell them so. This kind of contact may be better coming from the head of your organisation, on behalf of the whole organisation, rather than from an individual. Alternatively, many learning providers are part of consortia or associations, so a letter could be sent on behalf of a number of providers – the bigger the better.

Contact us

Share your case studies and any imaginative and innovative uses that you have found for using e-books and e-readers with your learners. We will include them in a follow-up guide and acknowledge you.

Sandie Gay: sandie.gay@gmail.com
Tina Richardson: t.a.richardson@staffs.ac.uk

Useful websites

Website	Link
AbilityNet has been a leading authority on accessibility and assistive technologies for 20 years. Free factsheets, helplines and online tools help people with a range of disabilities to tailor their IT to meet their needs.	www.abilitynet.org.uk
Bookeen is an e-reader with a high-speed ink system (HSIS), making it faster to 'turn' pages.	http://bookeen.com/en
Calibre is a free and open-source e-book library management application developed by users of e-books for users of e-books.	http://calibre-ebook.com/about
DAISY is software to create digital talking books.	www.daisy.org/daisypedia/daisy-digital-talking-book
Dotepub is a website where you can download web pages as an e-book.	http://dotepub.com
Electronic Frontier Foundation has produced a paper on 'digital books and your rights'.	https://www.eff.org
Excellence Gateway provides resources for teaching and learning in the lifelong learning sector	www.excellencegateway.org.uk
Flesch–Kincaid readability test is available here.	http://en.wikipedia.org/wiki/Flesch%E2%80%93Kincaid_readability_test
Flipsnack – create e-books from PDF documents.	www.flipsnack.com

Website	Link
Howjsay is an e-dictionary that says the words aloud to aid pronunciation.	www.howjsay.com
Intel Reader – provides text to speech.	www.intel.com/corporate/healthcare/emea/eng/reader/index.htm
iPads in education, using apps for teaching and learning.	www.iPadineducation.co.uk/iPad_in_Education/Welcome.html
JAWS – screen reading software for blind or partially sighted people.	www.freedomscientific.com/products/fs/jaws-product-page.asp
JISC provides an introduction to e-books.	www.jiscdigitalmedia.ac.uk/crossmedia/advice/introduction-to-e-books
JISC – e-books for FE Project. This collection of approximately 2,996 e-books is part of the 'e-books for FE' project. to provide taught course e-books for FE students and teachers.	www.jisc-collections.ac.uk/Catalogue/Overview/index/185
Mobi-pocket – e-books and e-book reader for your PC, PDA and smartphone	www.MOBIpocket.com/en/HomePage/default.asp?Language=EN
Newspaper index provides an online list of e-newspapers from around the world.	www.newspaperindex.com/
Overdrive is a selction of e-books for libraries – check to see if your local public library offers e-books.	www.overdrive.com
Publisher Lookup UK – find electronic formats of textbooks here.	www.publisherlookup.org.uk
Reading Agency – find a read – help to choose an e-book.	www.readingagency.org.uk/findaread

Website	Link
Reading Groups provide help and resources for emergent reading groups.	http://readinggroups.org
Rising Stars is a publishing website for paper-based resources for schools as well as software.	www.risingstars-uk.com
RNIB – text-to-speech information for e-books is available here.	www.rnib.org.uk/livingwithsightloss/ readingwriting/ebooks/pages/text_to_speech .aspx
RNIB – Right to Read campaign: The Right to Read Alliance campaigns to ensure that everyone can read the 'same book, the same time, the same price.'	www.rnib.org.uk/getinvolved/ campaign/accesstoinformation/righttoread/ Pages/righttoread.aspx
Sigil – free e-book developer.	http://code.google.com
Six Book Challenge – The Reading Agency.	www.sixbookchallenge.org.uk
SolarFocus is a solar cover for the Kindle, which means you can read in the dark and increase the battery life.	www.solarmio.com/en
Tefl.net is a great resource for English teachers.	www.tefl.net/links/Reading/Books/ index.htm
Which? guide to cheapest e-books is available here.	http://blogs.which.co.uk/technology/tablets-ebooks/who-sells-the-cheapest-ebooks
Which? guide to free e-books.	www.which.co.uk/technology/ computing/guides/find-and-download-free-ebooks
Worldreader – project to provide children in the developing world with e-books.	www.worldreader.org

Glossary

Acronym, abbreviation, word or phrase	Meaning	Explanatory information and source, if appropriate
Adult Core Curricula	Curricula documents developed for adult literacy, language and numeracy.	These can be found on the Excellence Gateway at: www.excellencegateway.org.uk/sflcurriculum
App	A software application.	In this case, for reading e-books on devices other than dedicated e-readers, e.g. iPad, smartphones or PCs
Copyright		To give the creator of an original work the exclusive right to it.
Digital literacy	Skills for using digital technologies and exploiting their potential.	From Wikipedia: Digital literacy is the ability to locate, organize, understand, evaluate, and analyze information using digital technology. It involves a working knowledge of current advanced technology and an understanding of how it can be used. http://en.wikipedia.org/wiki/Digital_literacy
DRM	Digital rights management.	Encoding used to restrict the use of digital content not intended by the content provider.
EPUB	E-book file format.	The open standards file format that is supported by many devices and apps as opposed to a restricted file format such as the proprietary .AZW for Kindles only.

Acronym, abbreviation, word or phrase	Meaning	Explanatory information and source, if appropriate
E-book/ E-magazine/ E-journal/ E-newspaper	Electronic book, magazine, journal or newspaper	A book, magazine, journal or newspaper in digital form that needs a computer or suitable electronic device to read it on.
E-ink screen	Display screen using electronic ink found on dedicated e-readers such as the Amazon Kindle and Sony Reader, and hybrid e-readers such as the Kobo Vox.	Specially designed to be anti-glare and therefore easy on the eyes when reading for a long time.
E-reader	Electronic reader.	A gadget or device designed exclusively to read e-books, e-magazines or e-newspapers on, for example, Kindle, Sony Reader, or Kobo.
E-reading device	Electronic reading device.	A gadget or device that you can read e-books on, but that also has other primary functions such as a phone or a tablet.
File format	An extension added to the name of a file to indicate the file type usually requiring specific software to open.	A way that information has been coded to be stored in a computer file. For example, .GIF (image type) or .DOC (Microsoft Word document type), .EPUB (e-book type) or .PDF (portable document format).
Hybrid device	Referring to an e-reader with additional functions.	Devices which are created as dedicated e-readers, but that also run other applications and multimedia, such as Kobo Vox or Kindle Fire.
JISC RSC	JISC Regional Support Centre.	A network of 12 JISC Regional Support Centres across the UK assists higher and further education

Acronym, abbreviation, word or phrase	Meaning	Explanatory information and source, if appropriate
		colleges and skills providers with information, advice and guidance in the strategic use of technologies to achieve their organisational goals.
Literacies	Digital literacy and social media literacy.	Digital literacy is the ability to locate, organise, understand, evaluate, and analyse information using digital technology.[20] Social media literacy[21] – includes: • Attention – multi-tasking • Participation – having the written literacy skills to take part • Collaboration – being able to take part in conjunction with other people • Network awareness – fluency in knowing what is available • Critical consumption – being able to understand who to trust and who not to trust.
Mobile devices	Also known as handheld devices.	Small portable computing gadgets such as smartphones and tablets.
PDF	Portable Document Format.	A file format that displays a document to a certain specification in terms of font, etc.
Piracy	An infringement of copyright by copying a film, book etc., without permission.	
Public domain	No longer in copyright.	Where intellectual property rights have expired, so are publicly available and can be copied without a problem.
Reflow	Text flows and wraps when resized.	Text flows onto the next line when it is made bigger.

20. http://en.wikipedia.org/wiki/Digital_literacy
21. http://www.educause.edu/ero/article/attention-and-other-21st-century-social-media-literacies

Acronym, abbreviation, word or phrase	Meaning	Explanatory information and source, if appropriate
Screen orientation	Portrait or landscape.	Which way the screen can be read or if can be read both ways.
Screen reader	Software to help interpret what is on the screen.	Can also be assistive technology to help someone blind or partially sighted to read the screen on a gadget.
Serif/sans serif	Text styles with and without serifs.	Example of a serif text style is Times New Roman and sans serif is Arial.
Shelf	Display of books on an e-reader.	Often used to mean that e-books are displayed on the device or application as if on book shelves rather than simply listing the titles in text form.
Smartphone	Mobile phones developed as multifunctional devices.	Mobile phones that also run apps and multimedia.
Synchronisation	Aligning devices and e-books.	Used in the context of e-books and e-readers, synchronisation allows the same e-book to be read from the same place on each device or app registered to the same account.
Tablet	Computers that are portable like laptops, but usually smaller and lighter.	Mostly (but not exclusively) used to refer to touch-screen single-panel devices without a visible keyboard, such as the iPad.
Touch screen		A touch screen allows you to operate a gadget by touching the screen with your finger or with a stylus.
TTS	Text to speech.	A text-to-speech system can convert text into spoken language either through hardware or software.

Acronym, abbreviation, word or phrase	Meaning	Explanatory information and source, if appropriate
WhisperSync	Amazon's proprietary technology.	Allows multiple Kindle devices registered to the same account to synchronise with each other.
WiFi	Wireless networking.	A wire-free standard that allows multiple devices to communicate without being physically connected.
3G	Third generation.	The third derivation of a mobile telephone network.

Features of popular e-readers available in the UK

The table below provides details of features included in popular e-readers currently available in the UK, plus the iPad as an example of a tablet computer, and the iPod and smartphones as examples of the smaller multifunctional devices capable of supporting e-books.

Please note: specific versions of specific brands were investigated for review; many other brands of e-readers and multifunctional devices are available and with newer versions which may include different and additional features. Information given is a guide only; there will be variation according to use.

Top five e-readers easily available at time of publication	Amazon			Sony	Kobo			Apple		Various
	Kindle	Kindle Keyboard	Kindle Touch	Reader PRS-T1	Kobo Vox	Kobo touch	Kobo WiFi	iPad	iPod touch	Smartphones
Physical features										
1 Screen size (inches)	6	6	6	6	7	6	6	10	3.5	Varies from 3–5
2 Screen type	E-ink	E-ink	E-ink	E-ink	FFS and colour (optimised for reading in bright light)	E-ink	E-ink	LED-backlit IPS LCD	LED-backlit IPS LCD	LED-backlit IPS LCD
3 Change screen - orientation	✓	✓	✗	✓	✓	✗	✗	✓	✓	✓

Top five e-readers easily available at time of publication	Amazon			Sony	Kobo			Apple		Various
	Kindle	Kindle Keyboard	Kindle Touch	Reader PRS-T1	Kobo Vox	Kobo touch	Kobo WiFi	iPad	iPod touch	Smartphones
4 Single or two-page screen view	✗	✗		Two/three column view	✔		✗	Via e-book apps functionality	Via e-book apps functionality	Via e-book apps functionality
5 Page turning	Click bars in frame		Touch screen	Touch screen	Navigation pad	Touch screen	Touch screen	Touch screen	Touch screen	Touch screen
6 Text input	Virtual keyboard navigable using D-pad controller in frame	Physical keyboard plus navigation using five-way controller in frame	Virtual keyboard – touch-screen navigation	Virtual keyboard – touch-screen navigation	Virtual keyboard – touch-screen navigation		Virtual keyboard navigable using pad screen navigation	Virtual keyboard – touch-screen navigation	Virtual keyboard – touch-screen navigation	Virtual keyboard – touch-screen navigation
7 Battery life (regular use). Changes with battery age	Up to three weeks (wireless on); up to one month (wireless off)	Up to three weeks (wireless on); up to two months (wireless off)		107 hours	Up to seven hours	Up to four weeks	Up to two weeks	Up to ten hours	n/s	n/s

	Top five e-readers easily available at time of publication	Amazon			Sony	Kobo			Apple		Various
		Kindle	Kindle Keyboard	Kindle Touch	Reader PRS-T1	Kobo Vox	Kobo touch	Kobo WiFi	iPad	iPod touch	Smartphones
	Built-in software										
8	Internet connection type	WiFi enabled	Two versions: WiFi enabled plus WiFi enabled and free 3G	Two versions: WiFi enabled plus WiFi enabled and free 3G	WiFi enabled	WiFi enabled			WiFi enabled	WiFi enabled	WiFi enabled
9	E-book file formats supported	.AZW (Kindle); .PDF, unprotected .MOBI; .HTML; .TXT, .DOC/.DOCX (through conversion)			Adobe DRM protected .EPUB; Adobe PDF. Unprotected .EPUB; .PDF; .TXT.	Books: .EPUB, including Adobe DRM-protected .EPUB	.EPUB; .PDF and .MOBI; .TXT; .HTML and .RTF; .CBZ and .CBR	.EPUB; .PDF	As per app	As per app	As per app

Top five e-readers easily available at time of publication	Amazon			Sony	Kobo			Apple		Various
	Kindle	Kindle Keyboard	Kindle Touch	Reader PRS-T1	Kobo Vox	Kobo touch	Kobo WiFi	iPad	iPod touch	Smartphones
10 Multimedia file formats supported	Audible, .MP3, JPEG, .GIF, .PNG, .BMP (through conversion)			.AAC; .MP3; JPEG; .GIF; .PNG; .BMP	.AAC; .MP3; 3GP; .MP4; .M4A; .FLAC; .OGG; .WAV; .MID; .WEBM; JPEG; .GIF; .PNG; .BMP		✖	Yes – plays music and video and views most image files. Audio: .MP3; .AAC Video: .MP4, .WAV		Yes – varies according to phone
11 E-books stores	Amazon online store*			Sony e-store and other e-book stores	Kobo e-store and other e-book stores			Apple's iTunes store		Various
12 E-book stores and ease of downloading e-books	Books for the Kindles are only available for download from Amazon. Direct access to Amazon store via WiFi and/or 3G where available. Add supported books/documents by connecting to computer and file transfer. Can			E-books from any e-book store in the supported formats.	E-books from any e-book store in the supported formats. Direct access to Kobo store via WiFi. Add supported books/documents by connecting to computer and file transfer			Direct access to the iBookstore via the iBooks app (requires an Apple ID). Access to iTunes e-book store via		Varies. Direct access to other e-books stores via the e-book app or file transfer

* At the time of writing, Waterstones published an agreement made with Amazon to sell the Kindles at its stores and Kindle e-books on its online store.

Top five e-readers easily available at time of publication	Amazon			Sony	Kobo			Apple		Various
	Kindle	Kindle Keyboard	Kindle Touch	Reader PRS-T1	Kobo Vox	Kobo touch	Kobo WiFi	iPad	iPod touch	Smartphones
E-book stores and ease of downloading e-books (cont.)	also send files to Amazon by email for adding and/or converting to supported format or install and use the 'Send to Kindle' option on computer			Direct access to Sony store via WiFi. Add supported books/ documents by connecting to computer and file transfer				connection to your computer. Other e-books or PDFs (unrestricted) can be added to the iBook app by emailing the file, accessing your emails on the iPad or iPod choosing the option to open the attachment in iBooks. Access to other e-books via the e-book app associated with other stores		
13 Add own documents	File transfer or send to Kindle on computer			File transfer by connecting to computer	File transfer by connecting to computer			Sync the device with Apple's iTunes store or email and open attachment in the app		As per app functionality

Top five e-readers easily available at time of publication	Amazon			Sony	Kobo			Apple		Various
	Kindle	Kindle Keyboard	Kindle Touch	Reader PRS-T1	Kobo Vox	Kobo touch	Kobo WiFi	iPad	iPod touch	Smartphones
14 Text to speech**	No (was available in second version, but removed since)	Yes (plus Voice Guide for menu items***)	✔	✘	✔		✘	In-built VoiceOver (available in 36 languages) works with e-books using the iBook app	In-built VoiceOver – fourth generation (available in 36 languages) works with e-books using the iBook app	TTS apps available for some phones
15 Options to change text/background colour and contrast		✘		✘	Limited colour inversion – classic/sepia/night mode; brightness adjustment		✘	Yes, via e-book apps functionality		Yes, via e-book apps functionality

** Whilst speakers may be built into the device, it is necessary for the TTS feature to be enabled by the publisher on the individual book.

*** Does not work compatibly with TTS or on Kindle Store accessed from the e-reader.

	Amazon			Sony	Kobo			Apple		Various
Top five e-readers easily available at time of publication	**Kindle**	**Kindle Keyboard**	**Kindle Touch**	**Reader PRS-T1**	**Kobo Vox**	**Kobo touch**	**Kobo WiFi**	**iPad**	**iPod touch**	**Smartphones**
16 Option to change font size	Eight sizes			Yes – eight sizes. Dual finger zoom	Yes – 42 sizes	Yes – 17 sizes	Yes – five sizes	Via e-book apps functionality	Via e-book apps functionality	Via e-book apps functionality
17 Option to change font style	Three styles			Seven styles	Seven styles	Seven styles (option to add your own font style)	Two styles	Via e-book apps functionality	Via e-book apps functionality	Via e-book apps functionality
18 Options for words per line and line spacing		✓		✗	✗	No (text alignment feature for right or justified alignment)	n/s	Via some apps; e.g., Stanza		Via some apps – depends on phone OS and app

	Top five e-readers easily available at time of publication	Amazon			Sony	Kobo			Apple		Various
		Kindle	Kindle Keyboard	Kindle Touch	Reader PRS-T1	Kobo Vox	Kobo touch	Kobo WiFi	iPad	iPod touch	Smartphones
19	Bookmarking		✓		✓		✓			✓	✓
20	Highlighting and annotation		✓		✓	✓	Yes (except for native PDFs)	✓	Via app. Plus can have notebook app for notes		Via app. Plus can have notebook app for notes
21	Dictionary option	Multi-language: English plus translations to German, French, Italian, Brazilian and Portuguese			Multi-language: two English (British & American) and translations from English to French, German, Spanish, Dutch and Italian	Only for books from the Kobo book store	Two types: 'Dictionary Selection' for books from the Kobo book store, and 'Look up' for all supported files except PDFs	Only for books from the Kobo book store	Via some apps or own browser facility		Via some apps or own browser facility
22	Search		✓		✓		✓		Via some apps		Via some apps

Top five e-readers easily available at time of publication	Amazon			Sony	Kobo			Apple		Various
	Kindle	Kindle Keyboard	Kindle Touch	Reader PRS-T1	Kobo Vox	Kobo touch	Kobo WiFi	iPad	iPod touch	Smartphones
23 Social networks/ communities		✔		✔		✔		Via e-book apps functionality		Via e-book apps functionality
24 Navigation	D-Pad and click bars	Click bars and five-way controller	Touch screen	Touch screen	Touch screen plus three buttons	Touch screen	D-pad	Touch screen		Touch screen
25 Storage capacity	2GB (up to 1,400 books)	4GB (up to 3,500 books)	4GB (up to 3,000 books)	2GB (1,200 books)	8GB (8,000 books)	1GB (1,000 books)	1,000 books	16GB, 32GB and 64GB	Varies	Varies per phone
26 Extra capacity	✖	✖	✖	Micro SD card slot	Micro SD card slot			✖	✖	n/s
27 Different language versions	English, German, French, Italian, Brazilian and Portuguese	English	English, German, French, Italian, Brazilian and Portuguese	n/s	English French, German, Dutch and Italian			Via e-book apps functionality		Via e-book apps functionality

Top five e-readers easily available at time of publication	Amazon			Sony	Kobo				Apple		Various
	Kindle	Kindle Keyboard	Kindle Touch	Reader PRS-T1	Kobo Vox	Kobo touch	Kobo WiFi		iPad	iPod touch	Smartphones
Extras	n/s	n/s	Experimental browser; X-ray feature for curated content	Stylus pen; personalisation of screen-saver – great for learning providers information and logo	Experimental browser; reading statistics (books and pages) email and apps. Reading Life function for reading statistics.	n/s	n/s		n/s		n/s

28

n/s No specific information found or available